S0-BDT-292

FREE Test Taking Tips DVD Offer

To help us better serve you, we have developed a Test Taking Tips DVD that we would like to give you for FREE. **This DVD covers world-class test taking tips that you can use to be even more successful when you are taking your test.**

All that we ask is that you email us your feedback about your study guide. Please let us know what you thought about it – whether that is good, bad or indifferent.

To get your **FREE Test Taking Tips DVD**, email freedvd@studyguideteam.com with "FREE DVD" in the subject line and the following information in the body of the email:

   a. The title of your study guide.

   b. Your product rating on a scale of 1-5, with 5 being the highest rating.

   c. Your feedback about the study guide. What did you think of it?

   d. Your full name and shipping address to send your free DVD.

If you have any questions or concerns, please don't hesitate to contact us at freedvd@studyguideteam.com.

Thanks again!

CBEST Math Test Preparation 2018 & 2019

CBEST Math Book & Math Practice Tests for the California Basic Educational Skills Math Test

Test Prep Books Math Prep Team

Table of Contents

Quick Overview

As you draw closer to taking your exam, effective preparation becomes more and more important. Thankfully, you have this study guide to help you get ready. Use this guide to help keep your studying on track and refer to it often.

This study guide contains several key sections that will help you be successful on your exam. The guide contains tips for what you should do the night before and the day of the test. Also included are test-taking tips. Knowing the right information is not always enough. Many well-prepared test takers struggle with exams. These tips will help equip you to accurately read, assess, and answer test questions.

A large part of the guide is devoted to showing you what content to expect on the exam and to helping you better understand that content. In this guide are practice test questions so that you can see how well you have grasped the content. Then, answer explanations are provided so that you can understand why you missed certain questions.

Don't try to cram the night before you take your exam. This is not a wise strategy for a few reasons. First, your retention of the information will be low. Your time would be better used by reviewing information you already know rather than trying to learn a lot of new information. Second, you will likely become stressed as you try to gain a large amount of knowledge in a short amount of time. Third, you will be depriving yourself of sleep. So be sure to go to bed at a reasonable time the night before. Being well-rested helps you focus and remain calm.

Be sure to eat a substantial breakfast the morning of the exam. If you are taking the exam in the afternoon, be sure to have a good lunch as well. Being hungry is distracting and can make it difficult to focus. You have hopefully spent lots of time preparing for the exam. Don't let an empty stomach get in the way of success!

When travelling to the testing center, leave earlier than needed. That way, you have a buffer in case you experience any delays. This will help you remain calm and will keep you from missing your appointment time at the testing center.

Be sure to pace yourself during the exam. Don't try to rush through the exam. There is no need to risk performing poorly on the exam just so you can leave the testing center early. Allow yourself to use all of the allotted time if needed.

Remain positive while taking the exam even if you feel like you are performing poorly. Thinking about the content you should have mastered will not help you perform better on the exam.

Once the exam is complete, take some time to relax. Even if you feel that you need to take the exam again, you will be well served by some down time before you begin studying again. It's often easier to convince yourself to study if you know that it will come with a reward!

Test-Taking Strategies

1. Predicting the Answer

When you feel confident in your preparation for a multiple-choice test, try predicting the answer before reading the answer choices. This is especially useful on questions that test objective factual knowledge. By predicting the answer before reading the available choices, you eliminate the possibility that you will be distracted or led astray by an incorrect answer choice. You will feel more confident in your selection if you read the question, predict the answer, and then find your prediction among the answer choices. After using this strategy, be sure to still read all of the answer choices carefully and completely. If you feel unprepared, you should not attempt to predict the answers. This would be a waste of time and an opportunity for your mind to wander in the wrong direction.

2. Reading the Whole Question

Too often, test takers scan a multiple-choice question, recognize a few familiar words, and immediately jump to the answer choices. Test authors are aware of this common impatience, and they will sometimes prey upon it. For instance, a test author might subtly turn the question into a negative, or he or she might redirect the focus of the question right at the end. The only way to avoid falling into these traps is to read the entirety of the question carefully before reading the answer choices.

3. Looking for Wrong Answers

Long and complicated multiple-choice questions can be intimidating. One way to simplify a difficult multiple-choice question is to eliminate all of the answer choices that are clearly wrong. In most sets of answers, there will be at least one selection that can be dismissed right away. If the test is administered on paper, the test taker could draw a line through it to indicate that it may be ignored; otherwise, the test taker will have to perform this operation mentally or on scratch paper. In either case, once the obviously incorrect answers have been eliminated, the remaining choices may be considered. Sometimes identifying the clearly wrong answers will give the test taker some information about the correct answer. For instance, if one of the remaining answer choices is a direct opposite of one of the eliminated answer choices, it may well be the correct answer. The opposite of obviously wrong is obviously right! Of course, this is not always the case. Some answers are obviously incorrect simply because they are irrelevant to the question being asked. Still, identifying and eliminating some incorrect answer choices is a good way to simplify a multiple-choice question.

4. Don't Overanalyze

Anxious test takers often overanalyze questions. When you are nervous, your brain will often run wild, causing you to make associations and discover clues that don't actually exist. If you feel that this may be a problem for you, do whatever you can to slow down during the test. Try taking a deep breath or counting to ten. As you read and consider the question, restrict yourself to the particular words used by the author. Avoid thought tangents about what the author *really* meant, or what he or she was *trying* to say. The only things that matter on a multiple-choice test are the words that are actually in the question. You must avoid reading too much into a multiple-choice question, or supposing that the writer meant something other than what he or she wrote.

5. No Need for Panic

It is wise to learn as many strategies as possible before taking a multiple-choice test, but it is likely that you will come across a few questions for which you simply don't know the answer. In this situation, avoid panicking. Because most multiple-choice tests include dozens of questions, the relative value of a single wrong answer is small. As much as possible, you should compartmentalize each question on a multiple-choice test. In other words, you should not allow your feelings about one question to affect your success on the others. When you find a question that you either don't understand or don't know how to answer, just take a deep breath and do your best. Read the entire question slowly and carefully. Try rephrasing the question a couple of different ways. Then, read all of the answer choices carefully. After eliminating obviously wrong answers, make a selection and move on to the next question.

6. Confusing Answer Choices

When working on a difficult multiple-choice question, there may be a tendency to focus on the answer choices that are the easiest to understand. Many people, whether consciously or not, gravitate to the answer choices that require the least concentration, knowledge, and memory. This is a mistake. When you come across an answer choice that is confusing, you should give it extra attention. A question might be confusing because you do not know the subject matter to which it refers. If this is the case, don't eliminate the answer before you have affirmatively settled on another. When you come across an answer choice of this type, set it aside as you look at the remaining choices. If you can confidently assert that one of the other choices is correct, you can leave the confusing answer aside. Otherwise, you will need to take a moment to try to better understand the confusing answer choice. Rephrasing is one way to tease out the sense of a confusing answer choice.

7. Your First Instinct

Many people struggle with multiple-choice tests because they overthink the questions. If you have studied sufficiently for the test, you should be prepared to trust your first instinct once you have carefully and completely read the question and all of the answer choices. There is a great deal of research suggesting that the mind can come to the correct conclusion very quickly once it has obtained all of the relevant information. At times, it may seem to you as if your intuition is working faster even than your reasoning mind. This may in fact be true. The knowledge you obtain while studying may be retrieved from your subconscious before you have a chance to work out the associations that support it. Verify your instinct by working out the reasons that it should be trusted.

8. Key Words

Many test takers struggle with multiple-choice questions because they have poor reading comprehension skills. Quickly reading and understanding a multiple-choice question requires a mixture of skill and experience. To help with this, try jotting down a few key words and phrases on a piece of scrap paper. Doing this concentrates the process of reading and forces the mind to weigh the relative importance of the question's parts. In selecting words and phrases to write down, the test taker thinks about the question more deeply and carefully. This is especially true for multiple-choice questions that are preceded by a long prompt.

9. Subtle Negatives

One of the oldest tricks in the multiple-choice test writer's book is to subtly reverse the meaning of a question with a word like *not* or *except*. If you are not paying attention to each word in the question, you can easily be led astray by this trick. For instance, a common question format is, "Which of the following is...?" Obviously, if the question instead is, "Which of the following is not...?," then the answer will be quite different. Even worse, the test makers are aware of the potential for this mistake and will include one answer choice that would be correct if the question were not negated or reversed. A test taker who misses the reversal will find what he or she believes to be a correct answer and will be so confident that he or she will fail to reread the question and discover the original error. The only way to avoid this is to practice a wide variety of multiple-choice questions and to pay close attention to each and every word.

10. Reading Every Answer Choice

It may seem obvious, but you should always read every one of the answer choices! Too many test takers fall into the habit of scanning the question and assuming that they understand the question because they recognize a few key words. From there, they pick the first answer choice that answers the question they believe they have read. Test takers who read all of the answer choices might discover that one of the latter answer choices is actually *more* correct. Moreover, reading all of the answer choices can remind you of facts related to the question that can help you arrive at the correct answer. Sometimes, a misstatement or incorrect detail in one of the latter answer choices will trigger your memory of the subject and will enable you to find the right answer. Failing to read all of the answer choices is like not reading all of the items on a restaurant menu: you might miss out on the perfect choice.

11. Spot the Hedges

One of the keys to success on multiple-choice tests is paying close attention to every word. This is never truer than with words like *almost*, *most*, *some*, and *sometimes*. These words are called "hedges" because they indicate that a statement is not totally true or not true in every place and time. An absolute statement will contain no hedges, but in many subjects, the answers are not always straightforward or absolute. There are always exceptions to the rules in these subjects. For this reason, you should favor those multiple-choice questions that contain hedging language. The presence of qualifying words indicates that the author is taking special care with his or her words, which is certainly important when composing the right answer. After all, there are many ways to be wrong, but there is only one way to be right! For this reason, it is wise to avoid answers that are absolute when taking a multiple-choice test. An absolute answer is one that says things are either all one way or all another. They often include words like *every*, *always*, *best*, and *never*. If you are taking a multiple-choice test in a subject that doesn't lend itself to absolute answers, be on your guard if you see any of these words.

12. Long Answers

In many subject areas, the answers are not simple. As already mentioned, the right answer often requires hedges. Another common feature of the answers to a complex or subjective question are qualifying clauses, which are groups of words that subtly modify the meaning of the sentence. If the question or answer choice describes a rule to which there are exceptions or the subject matter is complicated, ambiguous, or confusing, the correct answer will require many words in order to be expressed clearly and accurately. In essence, you should not be deterred by answer choices that seem excessively long. Oftentimes, the author of the text will not be able to write the correct answer without offering some qualifications and modifications. Your job is to read the answer choices thoroughly and completely and to select the one that most accurately and precisely answers the question.

13. Restating to Understand

Sometimes, a question on a multiple-choice test is difficult not because of what it asks but because of how it is written. If this is the case, restate the question or answer choice in different words. This process serves a couple of important purposes. First, it forces you to concentrate on the core of the question. In order to rephrase the question accurately, you have to understand it well. Rephrasing the question will concentrate your mind on the key words and ideas. Second, it will present the information to your mind in a fresh way. This process may trigger your memory and render some useful scrap of information picked up while studying.

14. True Statements

Sometimes an answer choice will be true in itself, but it does not answer the question. This is one of the main reasons why it is essential to read the question carefully and completely before proceeding to the answer choices. Too often, test takers skip ahead to the answer choices and look for true statements. Having found one of these, they are content to select it without reference to the question above. Obviously, this provides an easy way for test makers to play tricks. The savvy test taker will always read the entire question before turning to the answer choices. Then, having settled on a correct answer choice, he or she will refer to the original question and ensure that the selected answer is relevant. The mistake of choosing a correct-but-irrelevant answer choice is especially common on questions related to specific pieces of objective knowledge. A prepared test taker will have a wealth of factual knowledge at his or her disposal, and should not be careless in its application.

15. No Patterns

One of the more dangerous ideas that circulates about multiple-choice tests is that the correct answers tend to fall into patterns. These erroneous ideas range from a belief that B and C are the most common right answers, to the idea that an unprepared test-taker should answer "A-B-A-C-A-D-A-B-A." It cannot be emphasized enough that pattern-seeking of this type is exactly the WRONG way to approach a multiple-choice test. To begin with, it is highly unlikely that the test maker will plot the correct answers according to some predetermined pattern. The questions are scrambled and delivered in a random order. Furthermore, even if the test maker was following a pattern in the assignation of correct answers, there is no reason why the test taker would know which pattern he or she was using. Any attempt to discern a pattern in the answer choices is a waste of time and a distraction from the real work of taking the test. A test taker would be much better served by extra preparation before the test than by reliance on a pattern in the answers.

FREE DVD OFFER

Don't forget that doing well on your exam includes both understanding the test content and understanding how to use what you know to do well on the test. We offer a completely FREE Test Taking Tips DVD that covers world class test taking tips that you can use to be even more successful when you are taking your test.

All that we ask is that you email us your feedback about your study guide. To get your **FREE Test Taking Tips DVD**, email freedvd@studyguideteam.com with "FREE DVD" in the subject line and the following information in the body of the email:

- The title of your study guide.
- Your product rating on a scale of 1-5, with 5 being the highest rating.
- Your feedback about the study guide. What did you think of it?
- Your full name and shipping address to send your free DVD.

Introduction to the CBEST

Function of the Test

The California Basic Educational Skills Test (CBEST) was created by the government of the state of California as a way for teacher candidates to demonstrate proficiency in reading, writing, and mathematics. Individuals applying for their first California teaching credential, applying for admission to certain teacher preparation and credentialing programs, or seeking employment in a California school district or educational agency must meet the California Basic Skills Requirement. The California legislature has established eight different ways to meet this requirement, such as achieving certain scores on various tests, one of which is to pass the CBEST. The state of Nevada has also adopted the CBEST as a way to meet certain Nevada licensing requirements.

CBEST scores are generally used only for California and Nevada teacher licensing, credentialing and hiring. In the 2014-2015 school year, 32,890 individuals took the CBEST for the first time. 22,847 of these first-time test takers passed, for a passing rate of 69.5%. The passing rate over the last five years has ranged from 69.5% to 71.4%. Of the three sections, reading and math are generally a bit easier to pass, with passing rates of around 80%, while writing is a bit more difficult, with a passing rate around 73%. (http://www.ctc.ca.gov/commission/agendas/2016-04/2016-04-5C.pdf).

Test Administration

The computer-based version of the CBEST is offered year-round by appointment, Monday through Saturday, excluding certain holidays, at Pearson VUE testing centers. The paper-based version is available on a more limited basis, usually around five times per school year. Individuals who do not pass must wait 45 days to attempt the CBEST again on computer, or may attempt the test again on any scheduled paper-administered test day.

All CBEST test sites are wheelchair-accessible. Individuals with documented disabilities may receive additional accommodations such as allowance of a medical device in the testing room, additional breaks, and use of tools such as a magnifying glass or straight edge. Individuals seeking such accommodation should complete and submit an Alternative Testing Arrangements Request Form along with appropriate documentation prior to their scheduled test date. The form must be submitted each time a student seeking accommodations takes the CBEST exam.

Test Format

A CBEST testing session will last four hours. Test takers may elect to take one, two, or all three of the sections offered. The reading section is made up of questions designed to assess the test takers ability to comprehend information in written passages, tables, and graphs. The mathematics section is primarily comprised of word problems to be solved without the use of a calculator. The writing section is composed of two essays, one in which the test taker is asked to analyze a given situation or statement and one in which the test taker is asked to describe a personal experience

A summary of the content of the CBEST is as follows:

Section	Subsection	Approx # of Questions
Reading	Critical analysis and evaluation	20
	Comprehension and research skills	30
Mathematics	Estimation, measurement, and statistical principles	15
	Computation and problem solving	17
	Numerical and graphic relationships	17
Writing	Essay	2

Scoring

Scoring on the reading and math sections is done by calculating a raw score based on the number of correct answers with no penalty for guessing incorrectly and converting that raw score to a scaled score between 20 and 80. Similarly, the essays in the writing section are given a score between 1 and 4 by two readers for each of the two essays. The total raw score (between 4 and 16) is then converted to a scaled score between 20 and 80.

Test takers may pass the CBEST by *either* earning scaled score on each section of at least 41, *or* earning a scaled score on each section of at least 37 and a total scaled score of at least 123. As discussed above, the passing rate on individual sections ranges from the mid-70s to around 80%, and the overall passing rate hovers around 70%.

Estimation, Measurement, & Statistical Principles

Estimation and Measurement

Measurement Systems and Standard Units of Measure

The American Measuring System

The measuring system used today in the United States developed from the British units of measurement during colonial times. The most typically used units in this customary system are those used to measure weight, liquid volume, and length, whose common units are found below. In the customary system, the basic unit for measuring weight is the ounce (oz); there are 16 ounces (oz) in 1 pound (lb) and 2000 pounds in 1 ton. The basic unit for measuring liquid volume is the ounce (oz); 1 ounce is equal to 2 tablespoons (tbsp) or 6 teaspoons (tsp), and there are 8 ounces in 1 cup, 2 cups in 1 pint (pt), 2 pints in 1 quart (qt), and 4 quarts in 1 gallon (gal). For measurements of length, the inch (in) is the base unit; 12 inches make up 1 foot (ft), 3 feet make up 1 yard (yd), and 5280 feet make up 1 mile (mi). However, as there are only a set number of units in the customary system, with extremely large or extremely small amounts of material, the numbers can become awkward and difficult to compare.

Common Customary Measurements		
Length	**Weight**	**Capacity**
1 foot = 12 inches	1 pound = 16 ounces	1 cup = 8 fluid ounces
1 yard = 3 feet ✓	1 ton = 2,000 pounds	1 pint = 2 cups
1 yard = 36 inches		1 quart = 2 pints
1 mile = 1,760 yards		1 quart = 4 cups
1 mile = 5,280 feet		1 gallon = 4 quarts
		1 gallon = 16 cups

The Metric System

Aside from the United States, most countries in the world have adopted the metric system embodied in the International System of Units (SI). The three main SI base units used in the metric system are the meter (m), the kilogram (kg), and the liter (L); meters measure length, kilograms measure mass, and liters measure volume.

These three units can use different prefixes, which indicate larger or smaller versions of the unit by powers of ten. This can be thought of as making a new unit which is sized by multiplying the original unit in size by a factor.

These prefixes and associated factors are:

Metric Prefixes			
Prefix	Symbol	Multiplier	Exponential
giga	G	1,000,000,000	10^9
mega	M	1,000,000	10^6
kilo	k	1,000	10^3
hecto	h	100	10^2
deca	da	10	10^1
no prefix		1	10^0
deci	d	0.1	10^{-1}
centi	c	0.01	10^{-2}
milli	m	0.001	10^{-3}
micro	μ	0.000001	10^{-6}
nano	n	0.000000001	10^{-9}

The correct prefix is then attached to the base. Some examples:

      1 milliliter equals .001 liters.
      1,000,000,000 nanometers equals 1 meter.
      1 kilogram equals 1,000 grams.

Choosing the Appropriate Measuring Unit
Some units of measure are represented as square or cubic units depending on the solution. For example, perimeter is measured in units, area is measured in square units, and volume is measured in cubic units.

Also be sure to use the most appropriate unit for the thing being measured. A building's height might be measured in feet or meters while the length of a nail might be measured in inches or centimeters. Additionally, for SI units, the prefix should be chosen to provide the most succinct available value. For example, the mass of a bag of fruit would likely be measured in kilograms rather than grams or milligrams, and the length of a bacteria cell would likely be measured in micrometers rather than centimeters or kilometers.

Conversions
Converting measurements in different units between the two systems can be difficult because they follow different rules. The best method is to look up an English to Metric system conversion factor and then use a series of equivalent fractions to set up an equation to convert the units of one of the measurements into those of the other.

The table below lists some common conversion values that are useful for problems involving measurements with units in both systems:

English System	Metric System
1 inch	2.54 cm
1 foot	0.3048 m
1 yard	0.914 m
1 mile	1.609 km
1 ounce	28.35 g
1 pound	0.454 kg
1 fluid ounce	29.574 mL
1 quart	0.946 L
1 gallon	3.785 L

Consider the example where a scientist wants to convert 6.8 inches to centimeters. The table above is used to find that there are 2.54 centimeters in every inch, so the following equation should be set up and solved:

$$\frac{6.8 \; in}{1} \times \frac{2.54 \; cm}{1 \; in} = 17.272 \; cm$$

Notice how the inches in the numerator of the initial figure and the denominator of the conversion factor cancel out. (This equation could have been written simply as $6.8 \; in \times 2.54 \; cm = 17.272 \; cm$, but it was shown in detail to illustrate the steps). The goal in any conversion equation is to set up the fractions so that the units you are trying to convert from cancel out and the units you desire remain.

For a more complicated example, consider converting 2.15 kilograms into ounces. The first step is to convert kilograms into grams and then grams into ounces. Note that the measurement you begin with does not have to be put in a fraction.

So in this case, 2.15 kg is by itself although it's technically the numerator of a fraction:

$$2.15 \; kg \times \frac{1000g}{kg} = 2150 \; g$$

Then, use the conversion factor from the table to convert grams to ounces:

$$2150g \times \frac{1 \; oz}{28.35g} = 75.8 \; oz$$

Perimeter and Area

Perimeter is the measurement of a distance around something or the sum of all sides of a polygon. Think of perimeter as the length of the boundary, like a fence. In contrast, **area** is the space occupied by a defined enclosure, like a field enclosed by a fence.

When thinking about perimeter, think about walking around the outside of something. When thinking about area, think about the amount of space or **surface area** something takes up.

Squares

The perimeter of a square is measured by adding together all of the sides. Since a square has four equal sides, its perimeter can be calculated by multiplying the length of one side by 4. Thus, the formula is $P = 4 \times s$, where s equals one side. For example, the following square has side lengths of 5 meters:

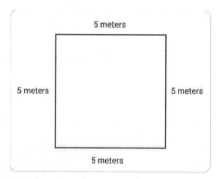

The perimeter is 20 meters because 4 times 5 is 20.

The area of a square is the length of a side squared, and the area of a rectangle is length multiplied by the width. For example, if the length of the square is 7 centimeters, then the area is 49 square centimeters. The formula for this example is $A = s^2 = 7^2 = 49$ square centimeters. An example is if the rectangle has a length of 6 inches and a width of 7 inches, then the area is 42 square inches:

$$A = lw = 6(7) = 42 \text{ square inches}$$

Rectangles

Like a square, a rectangle's perimeter is measured by adding together all of the sides. But as the sides are unequal, the formula is different. A rectangle has equal values for its lengths (long sides) and equal values for its widths (short sides), so the perimeter formula for a rectangle is:

$$P = l + l + w + w = 2l + 2w$$

l equals length
w equals width

The area is found by multiplying the length by the width, so the formula is $A = l \times w$.

For example, if the length of a rectangle is 10 inches and the width 8 inches, then the perimeter is 36 inches because:

$$P = 2l + 2w = 2(10) + 2(8) = 20 + 16 = 36 \text{ inches}$$

Triangles

A triangle's perimeter is measured by adding together the three sides, so the formula is $P = a + b + c$, where a, b, and c are the values of the three sides. The area is the product of one-half the base and height so the formula is:

$$A = \frac{1}{2} \times b \times h$$

It can be simplified to:

Triangle formula (handwritten)

$$A = \frac{bh}{2}$$

The base is the bottom of the triangle, and the height is the distance from the base to the peak. If a problem asks to calculate the area of a triangle, it will provide the base and height.

For example, if the base of the triangle is 2 feet and the height 4 feet, then the area is 4 square feet. The following equation shows the formula used to calculate the area of the triangle:

$$A = \frac{1}{2}bh = \frac{1}{2}(2)(4) = 4 \text{ square feet}$$

(handwritten calculations in right margin)
$$\frac{1}{2} \times \frac{2}{1} = 2$$
$$\frac{1}{2} \times \frac{4}{1} = \frac{4}{2} = 2$$
$$= 4$$

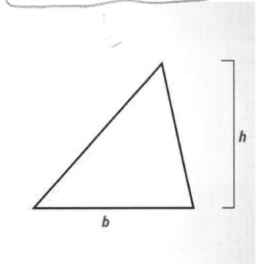

Circles
A circle's perimeter—also known as its circumference—is measured by multiplying the diameter by π.

Diameter is the straight line measured from one end to the direct opposite end of the circle.

π is referred to as pi and is equal to 3.14 (with rounding).

So the formula is $\pi \times d$.

This is sometimes expressed by the formula $C = 2 \times \pi \times r$, where r is the radius of the circle. These formulas are equivalent, as the radius equals half of the diameter.

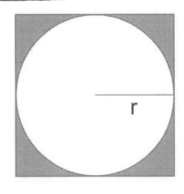

The area of a circle is calculated through the formula $A = \pi \times r^2$. The test will indicate either to leave the answer with π attached or to calculate to the nearest decimal place, which means multiplying by 3.14 for π.

Parallelograms

Similar to triangles, the height of the parallelogram is measured from one base to the other at a 90° angle (or perpendicular).

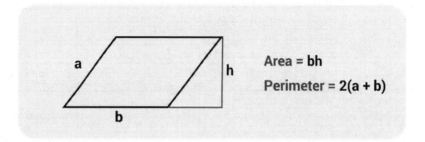

Area = bh

Perimeter = 2(a + b)

Trapezoid

The area of a trapezoid can be calculated using the formula: $A = \frac{1}{2} \times h(b_1 + b_2)$, where h is the height and b_1 and b_2 are the parallel bases of the trapezoid.

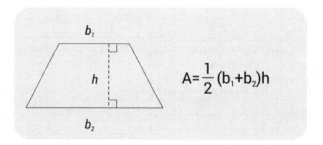

$$A = \frac{1}{2}(b_1 + b_2)h$$

Irregular Shapes

The perimeter of an irregular polygon is found by adding the lengths of all of the sides. In cases where all of the sides are given, this will be very straightforward, as it will simply involve finding the sum of the provided lengths. Other times, a side length may be missing and must be determined before the perimeter can be calculated. Consider the example below:

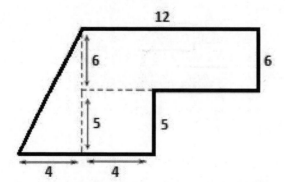

All of the side lengths are provided except for the angled side on the left. Test takers should notice that this is the hypotenuse of a right triangle. The other two sides of the triangle are provided (the base is 4

and the height is 6 + 5 = 11). The Pythagorean Theorem can be used to find the length of the hypotenuse, remembering that a² + b² = c².

Substituting the side values provided yields $(4)^2 + (11)^2 = c^2$.

Therefore, c = $\sqrt{16 + 121}$ = 11.7

Finally, the perimeter can be found by adding this new side length with the other provided lengths to get the total length around the figure: 4+4+5+8+6+12+11.7=50.7. Although units are not provided in this figure, remember that reporting units with a measurement is important.

The area of irregular polygons is found by decomposing, or breaking apart, the figure into smaller shapes. When the area of the smaller shapes is determined, the area of the smaller shapes will produce the area of the original figure when added together. Consider the earlier example:

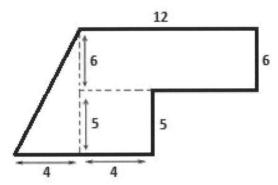

The irregular polygon is decomposed into two rectangles and a triangle. The area of the large rectangles ($A = l \times w \rightarrow A = 12 \times 6$) is 72 square units. The area of the small rectangle is 20 square units ($A = 4 \times 5$). The area of the triangle ($A = \frac{1}{2} \times b \times h \rightarrow A = \frac{1}{2} \times 4 \times 11$) is 22 square units. The sum of the areas of these figures produces the total area of the original polygon: $A = 72 + 20 + 22 \rightarrow A = 114$ square units.

Here's another example:

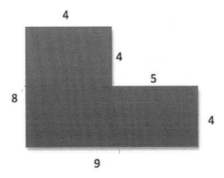

This irregular polygon is decomposed into two rectangles. The area of the large rectangle ($A = l \times w \rightarrow A = 8 \times 4$) is 32 square units. The area of the small rectangle is 20 square units ($A = 4 \times 5$). The sum of the areas of these figures produces the total area of the original polygon: $A = 32 + 20 \rightarrow A = 52$ square units.

Estimating Time

Estimation is finding a value that is close to a solution but is not the exact answer. For example, if there are values in the thousands to be multiplied, then each value can be estimated to the nearest thousand and the calculation performed. This value provides an approximate solution that can be determined very quickly.

When estimating, it's often convenient to **round** a number, which means to give an approximate figure to make it easier to compare amounts or perform mental math. Round up when the digit is 5 or more. The rounded The digit used to determine the rounding, and all subsequent digits, become 0, and the selected place value is increased by 1. Here are some examples:

> 75 rounded to the nearest ten is 80
> 380 rounded to the nearest hundred is 400
> 22.697 rounded to the nearest hundredth is 22.70

Round down when rounding on any digit that is below 5. The rounded digit, and all subsequent digits, becomes 0, and the preceding digit stays the same. Here are some examples:

> 92 rounded to the nearest ten is 90
> 839 rounded to the nearest hundred is 800
> 22.643 rounded to the nearest hundredth is 22.64

The same estimation strategies and techniques used when working with standard math problems can be employed when working with real-life situations. Estimation is frequently used in calculations involving money, such as for determining if one has enough money for a purchase, how much one needs to save weekly to buy a desired product, or how much a restaurant bill will sum to.

Another equally effective application of estimation—albeit a bit more difficult and less straightforward—involves time. Many people find it helpful to estimate the length of time it will take them to complete a given task or perform some function. This enables them to budget their time and energy effectively and develop a schedule or timeline by which projects and activities should be addressed. Estimating one's time is especially helpful for work-related objectives, to set reasonable expectations and meet required deadlines accordingly.

When estimating time, the same principles of rounding can be used, but now there is context behind the rounding. In other words, there is a specific meaning to what is being rounded (hours, minutes, seconds, days, etc.). This context needs to be considered when making the estimation and the rounding rules are typically not as formal and strict as those used in standard math calculations. For example, to round a number when performing regular mathematical calculations, the place value is specified. Then, as mentioned, the digit to its right is looked at. For example, if rounding to the nearest hundreds place, the digit in the tens place is used. If it is a 0, 1, 2, 3, or 4, the digit being rounded to is left alone. If it is a 5, 6, 7, 8 or 9, the digit being rounded to is increased by one. All other digits before the decimal point are then changed to zeros, and the digits in decimal places are dropped. In contrast, there are no explicitly defined rules for rounding time. Two people may round time differently or the same person might round the same time differently depending on the situation. For example, it is 1:10pm, one person may say it is "around 1" and another might say it is "going on 1:30." Similarly, if someone is going on vacation in 24 days, he or she might say the vacation is in three weeks. If, instead, that person has been dieting for that length of time but have not seen results, he or she may say, "I've been dieting for about a month and still haven't lost a pound!" Although some of these estimations are more accurate than others, since formal rules don't exist, none are necessarily "wrong."

In general, estimating time is more complicated than estimation involved in mathematical computations because it not only involves rounding numbers and the normal mathematical techniques, but also the awareness or forethought about how long a certain task will likely take to complete. For example, if working with a team to design a new logo for a company, one has to try to imagine the realistic, but potential, factors that will affect the projected timeline (i.e., How long might meetings take with the other team members? Will a compromise or agreement be reached easily or does there tend to be a lot of stubbornness surrounding one's idea? What is the process like for logo approval?).

With that said, as one becomes more experienced in a given job position or more self-aware over time, his or her ability to estimate the time needed for various work-related objectives or other life functions will improve. In these cases, time estimations can be instrumental in establishing functional schedules and realistic timelines.

Estimating Prior to Calculating

Prior to performing operations and calculating the answer to a problem involving addition, subtraction, multiplication, or division, it is helpful to estimate the result. Doing so will enable the test taker to determine whether his or her computed answer is logical within the context of a given problem and prevent careless errors. For example, it is unfortunately common under the pressure of a testing situation for test takers to inadvertently perform the incorrect operation or make a simple calculation error on an otherwise easy math problem. By quickly estimating the answer by eyeballing the numbers, rounding if needed, and performing some simple mental math, test takers can establish an approximate expected outcome before calculating the specific answer. The derived result after computation can then be evaluated by its nearness to the expected answer. This is performed by approximating given values to perform mental math. Numbers should be rounded to the nearest value possible to check the initial results.

As mentioned, sometimes when performing operations such as multiplying numbers, the result can be estimated by rounding. For example, to estimate the value of 11.2×2.01, each number can be rounded to the nearest integer. This will yield a result of 22.

Rounding numbers helps with estimation because it changes the given number to a simpler, although less accurate, number than the exact given number. Rounding allows for easier calculations, which estimate the results of using the exact given number. The accuracy of the estimate and ease of use depends on the place value to which the number is rounded. First, the place value is specified. Then, the digit to its right is looked at. For example, if rounding to the nearest hundreds place, the digit in the tens place is used. If it is a zero, one, 2, 3, or 4, the digit being rounded to is left alone. If it is a 5, 6, 7, 8 or 9, the digit being rounded to is increased by one. All other digits before the decimal point are then changed to zeros, and the digits in decimal places are dropped. If a decimal place is being rounded to, all digits that come after are just dropped. For example, if 845,231.45 was to be rounded to the nearest thousands place, the answer would be 845,000. The 5 would remain the same due to the 2 in the hundreds place. Also, if 4.567 were to be rounded to the nearest tenths place, the answer would be 4.6. The 5 increased to 6 due to the 6 in the hundredths place, and the rest of the decimal is dropped.

Mental math should always be considered as problems are worked through, and the ability to work through problems in one's head helps save time. If a problem is simple enough, such as $15 + 3 = 18$, it should be completed mentally. The ability to do this will increase once addition and subtraction in higher place values are grasped. Also, mental math is important in multiplication and division. The times tables multiplying all numbers from 1 to 12 should be memorized. This will allow for division within those numbers to be memorized as well. For example, we should know easily that $121 \div 11 = 11$ because it should be memorized that $11 \times 11 = 121$. Here is the multiplication table to be memorized:

x	1	2	3	4	5	6	7	8	9	10	11	12	13	14	15
1	1	2	3	4	5	6	7	8	9	10	11	12	13	14	15
2	2	4	6	8	10	12	14	16	18	20	22	24	26	28	30
3	3	6	9	12	15	18	21	24	27	30	33	36	39	42	45
4	4	8	12	16	20	24	28	32	36	40	44	48	52	56	60
5	5	10	15	20	25	30	35	40	45	50	55	60	65	70	75
6	6	12	18	24	30	36	42	48	54	60	66	72	78	84	90
7	7	14	21	28	35	42	49	56	63	70	77	84	91	98	105
8	8	16	24	32	40	48	56	64	72	80	88	96	104	112	120
9	9	18	27	36	45	54	63	72	81	90	99	108	117	126	135
10	10	20	30	40	50	60	70	80	90	100	110	120	130	140	150
11	11	22	33	44	55	66	77	88	99	110	121	132	143	154	165
12	12	24	36	48	60	72	84	96	108	120	132	144	156	168	180
13	13	26	39	52	65	78	91	104	117	130	143	156	169	182	195
14	14	28	42	56	70	84	98	112	126	140	154	168	182	196	210
15	15	30	45	60	75	90	105	120	135	150	165	180	195	210	225

The values along the diagonal of the table consist of **perfect squares**. A perfect square is a number that represents a product of two equal integers.

Estimating Absolute and Relative Error in the Numerical Answer to a Problem

Once a result is determined to be logical within the context of a given problem, the result should be evaluated by its nearness to the expected answer. This is performed by approximating given values to perform mental math. Numbers should be rounded to the nearest value possible to check the initial results.

Consider the following example: A problem states that a customer is buying a new sound system for their home. The customer purchases a stereo for $435, 2 speakers for $67 each, and the necessary cables for $12. The customer chooses an option that allows him to spread the costs over equal payments for 4 months. How much will the monthly payments be?

After making calculations for the problem, a student determines that the monthly payment will be $145.25. To check the accuracy of the results, the student rounds each cost to the nearest ten ($440 + 70 + 70 + 10$) and determines that the total is approximately $590. Dividing by 4 months gives an approximate monthly payment of $147.50. Therefore, the student can conclude that the solution of $145.25 is very close to what should be expected.

When rounding, the place-value that is used in rounding can make a difference. Suppose the student had rounded to the nearest hundred for the estimation. The result ($400 + 100 + 100 + 0 = 600$; $600 \div 4 = 150$) will show that the answer is reasonable, but not as close to the actual value as rounding to the nearest ten.

When considering the accuracy of estimates, the error in the estimated solution can be shown as absolute and relative. **Absolute error** tells the actual difference between the estimated value and the true, calculated value. The **relative error** tells how large the error is in relation to the true value. There may be two problems where the absolute error of the values (the estimated one and the calculated one) is 10. For one problem, this may mean the relative error in the estimate is very small because the estimated value is 15,000, and the true value is 14,990. Ten in relation to the true value of 15,000 is small: 0.06%. For the other problem, the estimated value is 50, and the true value is 40. In this case, the absolute error of 10 means a high relative error because the true value is smaller. The relative error is 10/40 = 0.25 or 25%.

Statistical Principles

Performing Arithmetic Operations on Basic Statistical Data

The field of statistics describes relationships between quantities that are related, but not necessarily in a deterministic manner. For example, a graduating student's salary will often be higher when the student graduates with a higher GPA, but this is not always the case. Likewise, people who smoke tobacco are more likely to develop lung cancer, but, in fact, it is possible for non-smokers to develop the disease as well. **Statistics** describes these kinds of situations, where the likelihood of some outcome depends on the starting data.

Descriptive statistics involves analyzing a collection of data to describe its broad properties such average (or mean), what percent of the data falls within a given range, and other such properties. An example of this would be taking all of the test scores from a given class and calculating the average test score. **Inferential statistics** attempts to use data about a subset of some population to make inferences about the rest of the population. An example of this would be taking a collection of students who received tutoring and comparing their results to a collection of students who did not receive tutoring, then using that comparison to try to predict whether the tutoring program in question is beneficial.

To be sure that inferences have a high probability of being true for the whole population, the subset that is analyzed needs to resemble a miniature version of the population as closely as possible. For this reason, statisticians like to choose random samples from the population to study, rather than picking a specific group of people based on some similarity. For example, studying the incomes of people who live in Portland does not tell anything useful about the incomes of people who live in Tallahassee.

Ratios and Proportions
A **ratio** is a comparison of two quantities in a particular order. Example: If there are 14 computers in a lab, and the class has 20 students, there is a student to computer ratio of 20 to 14, commonly written as 20:14. Ratios are normally reduced to their smallest whole number representation, so 20:14 would be reduced to 10:7 by dividing both sides by 2.

20:14 reduce 10:7

A **proportion** is a relationship between two quantities that dictates how one changes when the other changes. A direct proportion describes a relationship in which a quantity increases by a set amount for every increase in the other quantity, or decreases by that same amount for every decrease in the other quantity. Example: Assuming a constant driving speed, the time required for a car trip increases as the distance of the trip increases. The distance to be traveled and the time required to travel are directly proportional.

Inverse proportion is a relationship in which an increase in one quantity is accompanied by a decrease in the other, or vice versa. Example: the time required for a car trip decreases as the speed increases, and increases as the speed decreases, so the time required is inversely proportional to the speed of the car.

Solving for x in a Proportion

Solve for *x* in this proportion: $\frac{10}{15} = \frac{x}{30}$.

There are two ways to solve for *x*.

Method 1: Cross multiply; then, solve for x.

$$\frac{10}{15} = \frac{x}{30}$$

$$10(30) = 15(x)$$

$$300 = 15x$$

$$300 \div 15 = 15x \div 15$$

$$x = 20$$

Method 2: Notice that 30 is twice as much as 15, so *x* should be twice as much as 10. Therefore, *x* = 10 × 2 = 20.

Mean, Median, and Mode

The **center** of a set of data (statistical values) can be represented by its mean, median, or mode. These are sometimes referred to as **measures of central tendency**.

Mean

Suppose that you have a set of data points and some description of the general properties of this data need to be found.

The first property that can be defined for this set of data is the **mean**. This is the same as average. To find the mean, add up all the data points, then divide by the total number of data points. For example, suppose that in a class of 10 students, the scores on a test were 50, 60, 65, 65, 75, 80, 85, 85, 90, 100. Therefore, the average test score will be:

$$\frac{50 + 60 + 65 + 65 + 75 + 80 + 85 + 85 + 90 + 100}{10} = 75.5$$

The mean is a useful number if the distribution of data is normal (more on this later), which roughly means that the frequency of different outcomes has a single peak and is roughly equally distributed on both sides of that peak. However, it is less useful in some cases where the data might be split or where there are some **outliers**. Outliers are data points that are far from the rest of the data. For example, suppose there are 10 executives and 90 employees at a company. The executives make $1000 per hour, and the employees make $10 per hour.

Therefore, the average pay rate will be:

$$\frac{\$1000 \cdot 11 + \$10 \cdot 90}{100} = \$119 \; per \; hour$$

In this case, this average is not very descriptive since it's not close to the actual pay of the executives *or* the employees.

Median ✓

Another useful measurement is the **median**. In a data set, the median is the point in the middle. The middle refers to the point where half the data comes before it and half comes after, when the data is recorded in numerical order. For instance, these are the speeds of the fastball of a pitcher during the last inning that he pitched (in order from least to greatest):

90, 92, 93, 93, 95, 96, 97, 97, 97

There are nine total numbers, so the middle or *median* number in the 5th one, which is 95.

In cases where the number of data points is an even number, then the average of the two middle points is taken. In the previous example of test scores, the two middle points are 75 and 80. Since there is no single point, the average of these two scores needs to be found. The average is:

$$\frac{75 + 80}{2} = 77.5$$

The median is generally a good value to use if there are a few outliers in the data. It prevents those outliers from affecting the "middle" value as much as when using the mean.

Since an outlier is a data point that is far from most of the other data points in a data set, this means an outlier also is any point that is far from the median of the data set. The outliers can have a substantial effect on the mean of a data set, but usually do not change the median or mode, or do not change them by a large quantity. For example, consider the data set (3, 5, 6, 6, 6, 8). This has a median of 6 and a mode of 6, with a mean of $\frac{34}{6} \approx 5.67$. Now, suppose a new data point of 1000 is added so that the data set is now (3, 5, 6, 6, 6, 8, 1000). This does not change the median or mode, which are both still 6. However, the average is now $\frac{1034}{7}$, which is approximately 147.7. In this case, the median and mode will be better descriptions for most of the data points.

The reason for outliers in a given data set is a complicated problem. It is sometimes the result of an error by the experimenter, but often they are perfectly valid data points that must be taken into consideration.

Mode

One additional measure to define for *X* is the **mode.** This is the data point that appears most frequently. If two or more data points all tie for the most frequent appearance, then each of them is considered a mode. In the case of the test scores, where the numbers were 50, 60, 65, 65, 75, 80, 85, 85, 90, 100, there are two modes: 65 and 85.

A data set may have a single mode, multiple modes, or no mode. If different values repeat equally as often, multiple modes exist. If no value repeats, no mode exists. Consider the following data sets:

- A: 7, 9, 10, 13, 14, 14
- B: 37, 44, 33, 37, 49, 44, 51, 34, 37, 33, 44
- C: 173, 154, 151, 168, 155

Set A has a mode of 14. Set B has modes of 37 and 44. Set C has no mode.

The range of a data set is the difference between the highest and the lowest values in the set. The range can be considered the span of the data set. To determine the range, the smallest value in the set is subtracted from the largest value. The ranges for the data sets A, B, and C above are calculated as follows: A: $14 - 7 = 7$; B: $51 - 33 = 18$; C: $173 - 151 = 22$.

Changing all values of a data set in a consistent way produces predictable changes in the measures of the center and range of the set. A linear transformation changes the original value into the new value by either adding a given number to each value, multiplying each value by a given number, or both. Adding (or subtracting) a given value to each data point will increase (or decrease) the mean, median, and any modes by the same value. However, the range will remain the same due to the way that range is calculated. Multiplying (or dividing) a given value by each data point will increase (or decrease) the mean, median, and any modes, and the range by the same factor.

Consider the following data set, call it set P, representing the price of different cases of soda at a grocery store: $4.25, $4.40, $4.75, $4.95, $4.95, $5.15. The mean of set P is $4.74. The median is $4.85. The mode of the set is $4.95. The range is $0.90. Suppose the state passes a new tax of $0.25 on every case of soda sold. The new data set, set T, is calculated by adding $0.25 to each data point from set P. Therefore, set T consists of the following values: $4.50, $4.65, $5.00, $5.20, $5.20, $5.40. The mean of set T is $4.99. The median is $5.10. The mode of the set is $5.20. The range is $.90. The mean, median and mode of set T is equal to $0.25 added to the mean, median, and mode of set P. The range stays the same.

Now suppose, due to inflation, the store raises the cost of every item by 10 percent. Raising costs by 10 percent is calculated by multiplying each value by 1.1. The new data set, set I, is calculated by multiplying each data point from set T by 1.1. Therefore, set I consists of the following values: $4.95, $5.12, $5.50, $5.72, $5.72, $5.94. The mean of set I is $5.49. The median is $5.61. The mode of the set is $5.72. The range is $0.99. The mean, median, mode, and range of set I is equal to 1.1 multiplied by the mean, median, mode, and range of set T because each increased by a factor of 10 percent.

Quartiles and Percentiles

The **first quartile** of a set of data X refers to the largest value from the first ¼ of the data points. In practice, there are sometimes slightly different definitions that can be used, such as the median of the first half of the data points (excluding the median itself if there are an odd number of data points). The term also has a slightly different use: when it is said that a data point lies in the first quartile, it means it is less than or equal to the median of the first half of the data points. Conversely, if it lies *at* the first quartile, then it is equal to the first quartile.

When it is said that a data point lies in the **second quartile**, it means it is between the first quartile and the median.

The **third quartile** refers to data that lies between ½ and ¾ of the way through the data set. Again, there are various methods for defining this precisely, but the simplest way is to include all of the data that lie between the median and the median of the top half of the data.

Data that lies in the **fourth quartile** refers to all of the data above the third quartile.

Percentiles may be defined in a similar manner to quartiles. Generally, this is defined in the following manner:

If a data point lies *in the n-th percentile*, this means it lies in the range of the first n% of the data.

If a data point lies *at* the n-th percentile, then it means that n% of the data lies below this data point.

Standard Deviation

Given a data set X consisting of data points $(x_1, x_2, x_3, \ldots x_n)$, the **variance** of X is defined to be:

$$\frac{\sum_{i=1}^{n}(x_i - \bar{X})^2}{n}$$

This means that the variance of X is the average of the squares of the differences between each data point and the mean of X. In the formula, $\bar{X}$ is the mean of the values in the data set, and x_i represents each individual value in the data set. The sigma notation indicates that the sum should be found with n being the number of values to add together. $i = 1$ means that the values should begin with the first value. This formula is used when finding variance of a population. If the data set represents a sample of points taken from a larger set, then divide by $n - 1$ when finding variance.

Given a data set X consisting of data points $(x_1, x_2, x_3, \ldots x_n)$, the **standard deviation** of X is defined to be:

$$s_x = \sqrt{\frac{\sum_{i=1}^{n}(x_i - \bar{X})^2}{n}}$$

In other words, the standard deviation is the square root of the variance.

Both the variance and the standard deviation are measures of how much the data tend to be spread out. When the standard deviation is low, the data points are mostly clustered around the mean. When the standard deviation is high, this generally indicates that the data are quite spread out, or else that there are a few substantial outliers.

As a simple example, compute the standard deviation for the data set (1, 3, 3, 5). First, compute the mean, which will be $\frac{1+3+3+5}{4} = \frac{12}{4} = 3$. Now, find the variance of X with the formula:

$$\sum_{i=1}^{4}(x_i - \bar{X})^2 = (1-3)^2 + (3-3)^2 + (3-3)^2 + (5-3)^2 = -2^2 + 0^2 + 0^2 + 2^2 = 8$$

Therefore, the variance is $\frac{8}{4} = 2$. Taking the square root, the standard deviation will be $\sqrt{2}$.

Note that the standard deviation only depends upon the mean, not upon the median or mode(s). Generally, if there are multiple modes that are far apart from one another, the standard deviation will be high. A high standard deviation does not always mean there are multiple modes, however.

Choosing an Appropriate Measure of Central Tendency

Measures of central tendency, namely mean, median, and mode, describe characteristics of a set of data. Specifically, they are intended to represent a *typical* value in the set by identifying a central position of the set. Depending on the characteristics of a specific set of data, different measures of central tendency are more indicative of a typical value in the set.

When a data set is grouped closely together with a relatively small range and the data is spread out somewhat evenly, the mean is an effective indicator of a typical value in the set. Consider the following data set representing the height of sixth grade boys in inches: 61 inches, 54 inches, 58 inches, 63 inches, 58 inches. The mean of the set is 58.8 inches. The data set is grouped closely (the range is only 9 inches) and the values are spread relatively evenly (three values below the mean and two values above the mean). Therefore, the mean value of 58.8 inches is an effective measure of central tendency in this case.

When a data set contains a small number of values either extremely large or extremely small when compared to the other values, the mean is not an effective measure of central tendency. Consider the following data set representing annual incomes of homeowners on a given street: $71,000; $74,000; $75,000; $77,000; $340,000. The mean of this set is $127,400. This figure does not indicate a typical value in the set, which contains four out of five values between $71,000 and $77,000. The median is a much more effective measure of central tendency for data sets such as these. Finding the middle value diminishes the influence of outliers, or numbers that may appear out of place, like the $340,000 annual income. The median for this set is $75,000 which is much more typical of a value in the set.

The mode of a data set is a useful measure of central tendency for categorical data when each piece of data is an option from a category. Consider a survey of 31 commuters asking how they get to work with results summarized below.

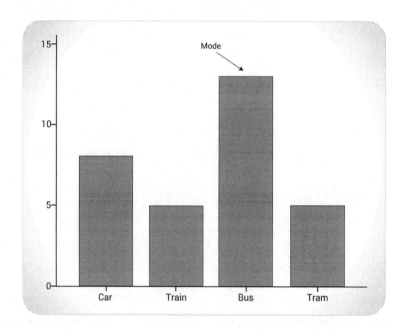

The mode for this set represents the value, or option, of the data that repeats most often. This indicates that the bus is the most popular method of transportation for the commuters.

Common Features of a Data Set
As mentioned, a set of data can be described in terms of its center, spread, shape and any unusual features. The center of a data set can be measured by its mean, median, or mode. The spread of a data set refers to how far the data points are from the center (mean or median). The spread can be measured by the range or the quartiles and interquartile range. A data set with data points clustered around the center will have a small spread. A data set covering a wide range will have a large spread.

When a data set is displayed as a histogram or frequency distribution plot, the shape indicates if a sample is normally distributed, symmetrical, or has measures of skewness or kurtosis. When graphed, a data set with a normal distribution will resemble a bell curve.

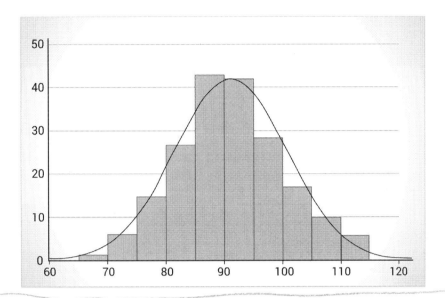

If the data set is **symmetrical**, each half of the graph when divided at the center is a mirror image of the other. If the graph has fewer data points to the right, the data is **skewed right**. If it has fewer data points to the left, the data is **skewed left**.

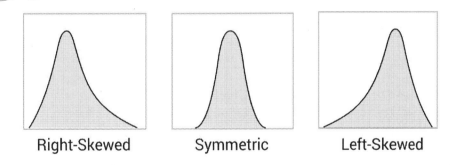

Right-Skewed   Symmetric   Left-Skewed

Kurtosis is a measure of whether the data is heavy-tailed with a high number of outliers, or light-tailed with a low number of outliers.

A description of a data set should include any unusual features such as gaps or outliers. A **gap** is a span within the range of the data set containing no data points. An **outlier** is a data point with a value either extremely large or extremely small when compared to the other values in the set.

The Basic Principles of Probability and Predicting the Likeliness of a Particular Outcome

Independent and Dependent Events

Probability is a measure of how likely an event is to occur. Probability is written as a fraction or decimal between zero and one. If an event has a probability of zero, the event will never occur. If an event has a probability of one, the event will definitely occur. If the probability of an event is closer to zero, the event is unlikely to occur. If the probability of an event is closer to one, the event is more likely to occur. For example, a probability of $\frac{1}{2}$ means that the event is equally as likely to occur as it is not to occur. An example of this is tossing a coin. To calculate the probability of an event, the number of favorable outcomes is divided by the number of total outcomes. For example, suppose you have 2 raffle tickets out of 20 total tickets sold. The probability that you win the raffle is calculated:

$$\frac{number\ of\ favorable\ outcomes}{total\ number\ of\ outcomes} = \frac{2}{20} = \frac{1}{10} \text{ (always reduce fractions)}$$

Therefore, the probability of winning the raffle is $\frac{1}{10}$ or 0.1.

Chance is the measure of how likely an event is to occur, written as a percent. If an event will never occur, the event has a 0% chance. If an event will certainly occur, the event has a 100% chance. If an event will sometimes occur, the event has a chance somewhere between 0% and 100%. To calculate chance, probability is calculated and the fraction is converted to a percent.

The probability of multiple events occurring can be determined by multiplying the probability of each event. For example, suppose you flip a coin with heads and tails, and roll a six-sided dice numbered one through six. To find the probability that you will flip heads AND roll a two, the probability of each event is determined and those fractions are multiplied. The probability of flipping heads is $\frac{1}{2}\left(\frac{1\ side\ with\ heads}{2\ sides\ total}\right)$ and the probability of rolling a two is $\frac{1}{6}\left(\frac{1\ side\ wit\ a\ 2}{6\ total\ sides}\right)$. The probability of flipping heads AND rolling a 2 is: $\frac{1}{2} \times \frac{1}{6} = \frac{1}{12}$.

The above scenario with flipping a coin and rolling a die is an example of independent events. Independent events are circumstances in which the outcome of one event does not affect the outcome of the other event. Conversely, dependent events are ones in which the outcome of one event affects the outcome of the second event. Consider the following scenario: a bag contains 5 black marbles and 5 white marbles. What is the probability of picking 2 black marbles without replacing the marble after the first pick?

The probability of picking a black marble on the first pick is $\frac{5}{10}\left(\frac{5\ black\ marbles}{10\ total\ marbles}\right)$. Assuming that a black marble was picked, there are now 4 black marbles and 5 white marbles for the second pick. Therefore, the probability of picking a black marble on the second pick is $\frac{4}{9}\left(\frac{4\ black\ marbles}{9\ total\ marbles}\right)$. To find the probability of picking two black marbles, the probability of each is multiplied:

$$\frac{5}{10} \times \frac{4}{9} = \frac{20}{90} = \frac{2}{9}$$

Conditional Probabilities

An outcome occasionally lies within some range of possibilities B, and the probability that the outcomes also lie within some set of possibilities A needs to be figured. This is called a **conditional probability**. It is written as $P(A|B)$, which is read "the probability of A given B." The general formula for computing conditional probabilities is:

$$P(A|B) = \frac{P(A \cap B)}{P(B)}$$

However, when dealing with uniform probability distributions, simplify this a bit. Write $|A|$ to indicate the number of outcomes in A. Then, for uniform probability distributions, write $P(A|B) = \frac{|A \cap B|}{|B|}$ (recall that $A \cap B$ means "A intersect B," and consists of all of the outcomes that lie in both A and B). This means that all possible outcomes do not need to be known. To see why this formula works, suppose that the set of outcomes X is $(x_1, x_2, x_3, \ldots x_n)$, so that $|X| = n$. Then, for a uniform probability distribution, $P(A) = \frac{|A|}{n}$. However, this means:

$$(A|B) = \frac{P(A \cap B)}{P(B)} = \frac{\frac{|A \cap B|}{n}}{\frac{|B|}{n}} = \frac{|A \cap B|}{|B|}$$

(since the n's cancel out)

For example, suppose a die is rolled and it is known that it will land between 1 and 4. However, how many sides the die has is unknown. Figure the probability that the die is rolled higher than 2. To figure this, $P(3)$ or $P(4)$ does not need to be determined, or any of the other probabilities, since it is known that a fair die has a uniform probability distribution. Therefore, apply the formula $\frac{|A \cap B|}{|B|}$. So, in this case B is $(1, 2, 3, 4)$ and $A \cap B$ is $(3, 4)$. Therefore:

$$\frac{|A \cap B|}{|B|} = \frac{2}{4} = \frac{1}{2}$$

Conditional probability is an important concept because, in many situations, the likelihood of one outcome can differ radically depending on how something else comes out. The probability of passing a test given that one has studied all of the material is generally much higher than the probability of passing a test given that one has not studied at all. The probability of a person having heart trouble is much lower if that person exercises regularly. The probability that a college student will graduate is higher when his or her SAT scores are higher, and so on. For this reason, there are many people who are interested in conditional probabilities.

Note that in some practical situations, changing the order of the conditional probabilities can make the outcome very different. For example, the probability that a person with heart trouble has exercised regularly is quite different than the probability that a person who exercises regularly will have heart trouble. The probability of a person receiving a military-only award, given that he or she is or was a soldier, is generally not very high, but the probability that a person being or having been a soldier, given that he or she received a military-only award, is 1.

However, in some cases, the outcomes do not influence one another this way. If the probability of A is the same regardless of whether B is given; that is, if $P(A|B) = P(A)$, then A and B are considered **independent**. In this case:

$$P(A|B) = \frac{P(A \cap B)}{P(B)} = P(A)$$

So:

$$P(A \cap B) = P(A)P(B)$$

In fact, if $P(A \cap B) = P(A)P(B)$, it can be determined that $P(A|B) = P(A)$ and $P(A|B) = P(B)$ by working backward. Therefore, B is also independent of A.

An example of something being independent can be seen in rolling dice. In this case, consider a red die and a green die. It is expected that when the dice are rolled, the outcome of the green die should not depend in any way on the outcome of the red die. Or, to take another example, if the same die is rolled repeatedly, then the next number rolled should not depend on which numbers have been rolled previously. Similarly, if a coin is flipped, then the next flip's outcome does not depend on the outcomes of previous flips.

This can sometimes be counterintuitive, since when rolling a die or flipping a coin, there can be a streak of surprising results. If, however, it is known that the die or coin is fair, then these results are just the result of the fact that over long periods of time, it is very likely that some unlikely streaks of outcomes will occur. Therefore, avoid making the mistake of thinking that when considering a series of independent outcomes, a particular outcome is "due to happen" simply because a surprising series of outcomes has already been seen.

There is a second type of common mistake that people tend to make when reasoning about statistical outcomes: the idea that when something of low probability happens, the outcome is surprising. It would be surprising that something with low probability happened after just one attempt. However, with so much happening all at once, it is easy to see at least something happen in a way that seems to have a very low probability. In fact, a lottery is a good example. The odds of winning a lottery are very small, but the odds that somebody wins the lottery each week are actually fairly high. Therefore, no one should be surprised when some low probability things happen.

Addition Rule
The **addition rule** for probabilities states that the probability of A or B happening is $P(A \cup B) = P(A) + P(B) - P(A \cap B)$. Note that the subtraction of $P(A \cap B)$ must be performed, or else it would result in double counting any outcomes that lie in both A and in B. For example, suppose that a 20-sided die is being rolled. Fred bets that the outcome will be greater than 10, while Helen bets that it will be greater than 4 but less than 15. What is the probability that at least one of them is correct?

We apply the rule $P(A \cup B) = P(A) + P(B) - P(A \cap B)$, where A is that outcome x is in the range $x > 10$, and B is that outcome x is in the range:

$$4 < x < 15. \ P(A) = 10 \cdot \frac{1}{20} = \frac{1}{2}. \ P(B) = 10 \cdot \frac{1}{20} = \frac{1}{2}$$

$P(A \cap B)$ can be computed by noting that $A \cap B$ means the outcome x is in the range $10 < x < 15$, so $P(A \cap B) = 4 \cdot \frac{1}{20} = \frac{1}{5}$.

Therefore:

$$P(A \cup B) = P(A) + P(B) - P(A \cap B) = \frac{1}{2} + \frac{1}{2} - \frac{1}{5} = \frac{4}{5}$$

Note that in this particular example, we could also have directly reasoned about the set of possible outcomes $A \cup B$, by noting that this would mean that x must be in the range $5 \leq x$. However, this is not always the case, depending on the given information.

Multiplication Rule

The **multiplication rule** for probabilities states the probability of A and B both happening is $P(A \cap B) = P(A)P(B|A)$. As an example, suppose that when Jamie wears black pants, there is a ½ probability that she wears a black shirt as well, and that she wears black pants ¾ of the time. What is the probability that she is wearing both a black shirt and black pants?

To figure this, use the above formula, where A will be "Jamie is wearing black pants," while B will be "Jamie is wearing a black shirt." It is known that $P(A)$ is ¾. It is also known that $P(B|A) = \frac{1}{2}$. Multiplying the two, the probability that she is wearing both black pants and a black shirt is $P(A)P(B|A) = \frac{3}{4} \cdot \frac{1}{2} = \frac{3}{8}$.

Counting Techniques

There are many counting techniques that can help solve problems involving counting possibilities; the Addition Principle and Multiplication Principle just described are two examples. Counting techniques also involve permutations. A **permutation** is an arrangement of elements in a set for which order must be considered. For example, if three letters from the alphabet are chosen, ABC and BAC are two different permutations. The multiplication rule can be used to determine the total number of possibilities. If each letter can't be selected twice, the total number of possibilities is $26 \times 25 \times 24 = 15,600$. A formula can also be used to calculate this total. In general, the notation $P(n, r)$ represents the number of ways to arrange r objects from a set of n and, the formula is $P(n, r) = \frac{n!}{(n-r)!}$. In the previous example, $P(26, 3) = \frac{26!}{23!} = 15,600$. Contrasting permutations, a **combination** is an arrangement of elements in which order doesn't matter. In this case, ABC and BAC are the same combination. In the previous scenario, there are six permutations that represent each single combination. Therefore, the total number of possible combinations is $15,600 \div 6 = 2,600$. In general, $C(n, r)$ represents the total number of combinations of n items selected r at a time where order doesn't matter, and the formula is:

$$C(n, r) = \frac{n!}{(n - r)! \, r!}$$

Therefore, the following relationship exists between permutations and combinations:

$$C(n, r) = \frac{P(n, r)}{n!} = \frac{P(n, r)}{P(r, r)}$$

Probability for an event is equal to the number of outcomes in that event divided by the total number of outcomes in the sample space. For example, consider rolling a 6-sided die. The probability of rolling an odd number is $\frac{3}{6}$, or $\frac{1}{2}$, because there are 3 odd numbers on the die.

The **fundamental counting principle** states that if there are m possible ways for an event to occur, and n possible ways for a second event to occur, there are $m \times n$ possible ways for both events to occur. For example, there are two events that can occur after flipping a coin and six events that can occur after rolling a die, so there are $2 \times 6 = 12$ total possible event scenarios if both are done simultaneously. This principle can be used to find probabilities involving finite sample spaces and independent trials because it calculates the total number of possible outcomes. For this principle to work, the events must be independent of each other.

Using Normal, Binomial, and Exponential Distributions
A **normal distribution** of data follows the shape of a bell curve and the data set's median, mean, and mode are equal. Therefore, 50 percent of its values are less than the mean and 50 percent are greater than the mean. Data sets that follow this shape can be generalized using normal distributions. Normal distributions are described as **frequency distributions** in which the data set is plotted as percentages rather than true data points. A **relative frequency distribution** is one where the y-axis is between zero and 1, which is the same as 0% to 100%. Within a standard deviation, 68 percent of the values are within 1 standard deviation of the mean, 95 percent of the values are within 2 standard deviations of the mean, and 99.7 percent of the values are within 3 standard deviations of the mean. The number of standard deviations that a data point falls from the mean is called the **z-score**. The formula for the z-score is $Z = \frac{x-\mu}{\sigma}$, where μ is the mean, σ is the standard deviation, and x is the data point. This formula is used to fit any data set that resembles a normal distribution to a standard normal distribution, in a process known as **standardizing**.

Here is a normal distribution with labeled z-scores:

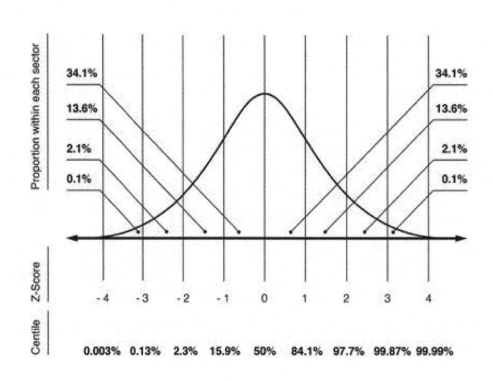

Normal Distribution with Labelled Z-Scores

Population percentages can be estimated using normal distributions. For example, the probability that a data point will be less than the mean, or that the z-score will be less than 0, is 50%. Similarly, the probability that a data point will be within 1 standard deviation of the mean, or that the z-score will be between -1 and 1, is about 68.2%. When using a table, the left column states how many standard deviations (to one decimal place) away from the mean the point is, and the row heading states the second decimal place. The entries in the table corresponding to each column and row give the probability, which is equal to the area.

In statistics, a **binomial experiment** is an experiment that has the following properties. The experiment consists of n repeated trial that can each have only one of two outcomes. It can be either a success or a failure. The probability of success, p, is the same in every trial. Each trial is also independent of all other trials. An example of a binomial experiment is rolling a die 10 times with the goal of rolling a 5. Rolling a 5 is a success while any other value is a failure. In this experiment, the probability of rolling a 5 is $\frac{1}{6}$. In any binomial experiment, x is the number of resulting successes, n is the number of trials, p is the probability of success in each trial, and $q = 1 - p$ is the probability of failure within each trial.

The probability of obtaining x successes within n trials is:

$$P(X = x) = \frac{n!}{x!\,(n-x)!} p^x (1-p)^{n-x}$$

With the following being the **binomial coefficient**:

$$\binom{n}{x} = \frac{n!}{x!\,(n-x)!}$$

Within this calculation, $n!$ is n factorial that's defined as:

$$n \times (n-1) \times (n-2) \dots 1$$

Let's look at the probability of obtaining 2 rolls of a 5 out of the 10 rolls.

Start with $P(X = 2)$, where 2 is the number of successes. Then fill in the rest of the formula with what is known, $n=10$, $x=2$, $p=1/6$, $q=5/6$:

$$P(X = 2) = \left(\frac{10!}{2!\,(10-2)!}\right)\left(\frac{1}{6}\right)^2\left(1-\frac{1}{6}\right)^{10-2}$$

Which simplifies to:

$$P(X = 2) = \left(\frac{10!}{2!\,8!}\right)\left(\frac{1}{6}\right)^2\left(\frac{5}{6}\right)^8$$

Then solve to get:

$$P(X = 2) = \left(\frac{3628800}{80640}\right)(.0277)(.2325) = .2898$$

A continuous random variable x is said to have an exponential distribution if it has probability density function $f(x) = \frac{1}{\beta}e^{-(x-\mu)/\beta}, x \geq \mu; \beta > 0$.

The value μ is known as the **location parameter**, and β is the **scale parameter**. Oftentimes, the scale parameter is referred to as λ and is equal to $^1/_\beta$. λ is also referred to as the scale parameter. When $\mu = 0$ and $\beta = 1$, this function is known as the **standard exponential distribution**, and $f(x) = e^{-x}$ for $x \geq 0$. Here is the plot of the exponential probability distribution function:

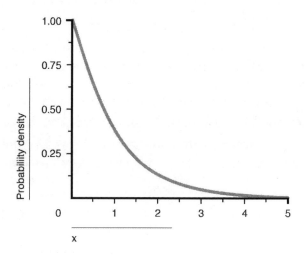

Similarly, the formula for the cumulative distribution function of the exponential function is $F(x) = 1 - e^{-x/\beta}$ for $x \geq 0, \beta > 0$, and here is its plot:

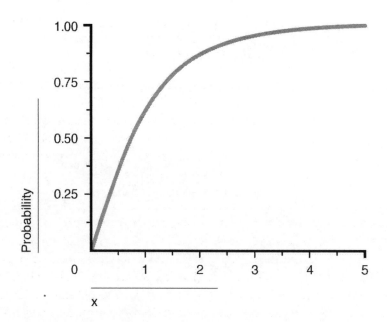

In probability and statistics, exponential distributions are used when the time between events that occur continuously and independently is a constant, average rate. The mean of an exponential distribution is $\beta = \frac{1}{\lambda}$, and its variance is $\beta^2 = \frac{1}{\lambda^2}$. Therefore, if the square root of the variance is taken, it is equal to the mean. Therefore, the standard deviation is equal to the mean.

Consider a rental car counter in which customers arrive at the rate of 20 per hour. The cumulative exponential distribution can be used to find the probability in which the arrival time between consecutive customers is less than 2 minutes. The mean number of customers per hour is 20, and therefore this is the rate of the function, so $\lambda = 20$. Two minutes represents 0.033 hour. Therefore, P(arrival time less than 2 minutes) = $1 - e^{-(20)(0.033)} = 0.483$. Therefore, there is a 48.3% chance that the arrival time between consecutive customers is less than 2 minutes.

Calculating Expected Values

The **expected value** of a random variable represents the mean value in either a large sample size or after a large number of trials. According to the law of large numbers, after a large number of trials, the actual mean (and that of the probability distribution) is approximately equal to the expected value. The expected value is a weighted average and is calculated as $E(X) = \sum x_i p_i$, where x_i represents the value of each outcome and p_i represents the probability of each outcome. If all probabilities are equal, the expected value is $E(X) = \frac{x_1 + x_2 + \cdots + x_n}{n}$. Expected value is often called the **mean of the random variable** and is also a measure of central tendency.

Consider the following situation: A landscaper bids on jobs where she can make a $2,000 profit. The probabilities of getting 1, 2, or 3 jobs per month are shown below in the probability distribution:

Number of Jobs	1	2	3
Probability	0.4	0.5	0.1

Her expected profit per month can be calculated by using the expected value formula. Multiply each probability times the profit in each instance, and sum up those values. This results in the following:

$$E(x) = 2,000 \times 0.4 + 4,000 \times 0.5 + 6,000 \times 0.1 = 800 + 2,000 + 600 = 3400$$

Therefore, she expects to make, on average, $3,400 per month.

Given a statistical experiment, a theoretical probability distribution can be calculated if the theoretical probabilities are known. The theoretical probabilities are plugged into the formula for both the binomial probability and the expected value. An example of this is any scenario involving rolls of a die or flips of a coin. The theoretical probabilities are known without any observed experiments. Another example of this is finding the theoretical probability distribution for the number of correct answers obtained by guessing a specific number of multiple choice questions on a class exam.

Empirical data is defined as real data. If real data is known, approximations concerning samples and populations can be obtained by working backwards. This scenario is the case where theoretical probabilities are unknown, and experimental data must be used to make decisions. The sample data (including actual probabilities) must be plugged into the formulas for both binomial probability and the expected value. The actual probabilities are obtained using observation and can be seen in a probability distribution. An example of this scenario is determining a probability distribution for the number of televisions per household in the United States, and determining the expected number of televisions per household as well.

Calculating if it's worth it to play a game or make a decision is a critical part of probability theory. Expected values can be calculated in terms of payoff values and deciding whether to make a decision or play a game can be done based on the actual expected value. Applying this theory to gambling and card games is fairly typical. The payoff values in these instances are the actual monetary totals.

Understanding Standardized Test Scores

Students will undoubtedly take several standardized tests throughout their academic career, and it is important for educators to be able to interpret results from these types of exams. Educators should be able to understand an individual student's score relative to the performance of his or her peer group, other students, or the aggregate of all test takers. Moreover, it is helpful to be able to explain this relative evaluation to inquisitive students, parents, and also school administrators. Many schools use their students' standardized test scores as a benchmark of performance for the school's curriculum and instruction in that content area. Additionally, with the importance of standardized test scores in competitive college admissions, many students and parents will likely have questions about scores that educators should be able to answer.

Standardized tests often make use of stanines, percentiles, or "grade-level equivalents" as means to compare an individual student's scores with the other students who attempted the exam. **Stanine** is a portmanteau for "standard nine" because the scores range from the minimum of 1 to the maximum of 9. This number range is further divided into three categories, which qualify an individual's performance relative to group at large. A stanine score of 1, 2, or 3 indicates that the student's raw score was "below average." Obtaining a stanine score of 4, 5, or 6 lands one in the "average" group, and scores of 7, 8, or 9 indicate an "above average" performance. Below average scores may indicate the need for further instruction and practice, and average scores mean that the student is at the same level as the majority of his or her peers.

Percentile scores delve into score comparisons with finer detail than stanine scores because instead of working on gross scale of 1-9, percentile scores range from 1 to 99. This multiplicative delineation of one's relative score allows for a significantly more precise performance comparison. A student's percentile score indicates the percentage of total test takers for whom that student outperformed. For example, a student who scored in the 77th percentile achieved a score that is higher than 77% of the rest of the test cohort. A student's percentile score is different than the percentage of correct responses obtained on the test. Percentile score simply compares one student's score with the scores of all of the other students who took the test. Students whose percentile scores fall below the 50th percentile can be considered below average, as more than half of the other test takers outperformed their test attempt.

Lastly, **grade-level equivalents** are sometimes used in situations where an exam is designed to be at the complexity or competency expected of a certain grade level but is taken by students in other grades. Because students at higher and lower grades than the test's intended grade attempt the exam, it can be challenging to interpret grade-level equivalents. Grade-level equivalents fall along a continuum and are often decimal results. The number to the right of the decimal approximates the number of months into that grade level (to the left of the decimal) for which a student's performance is on par. The school year is assumed to be ten months. For example, a score of 5.2 achieved by a fourth-grade student indicates that his or her raw score was that which a typical fifth grade student would receive two months into the school year.

Computation & Problem Solving

Basic Addition, Subtraction, Multiplication, and Division

Gaining more of something related to addition, while taking something away relates to subtraction. Vocabulary words such as *total*, *more, less, left*, and *remain* are common when working with these problems. The $+$ sign means plus. This shows that addition is happening. The $-$ sign means minus. This shows that subtraction is happening. The symbols will be important when you write out equations.

Addition
Addition can also be defined in equation form. For example, $4 + 5 = 9$ shows that $4 + 5$ is the same as 9. Therefore, $9 = 9$, and "four plus five equals nine." When two quantities are being added together, the result is called the **sum**. Therefore, the sum of 4 and 5 is 9. The numbers being added, such as 4 and 5, are known as the ***addends.***

Subtraction
Subtraction can also be in equation form. For example, $9 - 5 = 4$ shows that $9 - 5$ is the same as 4 and that "9 minus 5 is 4." The result of subtraction is known as a **difference**. The difference of $9 - 5$ is 4. 4 represents the amount that is left once the subtraction is done. The order in which subtraction is completed does matter. For example, $9 - 5$ and $5 - 9$ do not result in the same answer. $5 - 9$ results in a negative number. So, subtraction does not adhere to the commutative or associative property. The order in which subtraction is completed is important.

Multiplication
Multiplication is when we add equal amounts. The answer to a multiplication problem is called a **product**. Products stand for the total number of items within different groups. The symbol for multiplication is $\times$ or $\cdot$. We say 2×3 or $2 \cdot 3$ means "2 times 3."

As an example, there are three sets of four apples. The goal is to know how many apples there are in total. Three sets of four apples gives $4 + 4 + 4 = 12$. Also, three times four apples gives $3 \times 4 = 12$. Therefore, for any whole numbers a and b, where a is not equal to zero, $a \times b = b + b + \cdots b$, where b is added a times. Also, $a \times b$ can be thought of as the number of units in a rectangular block consisting of a rows and b columns. For example, 3×7 is equal to the number of squares in the following rectangle:

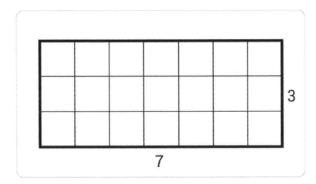

The answer is 21, and there are 21 squares in the rectangle.

With any number times one (for example, $8 \times 1 = 8$) the original amount does not change. Therefore, one is the **multiplicative identity**. For any whole number a, $1 \times a = a$. Also, any number multiplied times zero results in zero. Therefore, for any whole number a, $0 \times a = 0$.

Another method of multiplication can be done with the use of an **area model**. An area model is a rectangle that is divided into rows and columns that match up to the number of place values within each number. For example, $29 \times 65 = 25 + 4$ and $66 = 60 + 5$. The products of those 4 numbers are found within the rectangle and then summed up to get the answer. The entire process is:

$$(60 \times 25) + (5 \times 25) + (60 \times 4) + (5 \times 4) = 1{,}500 + 240 + 125 + 20 = 1{,}885.$$

Here is the actual area model:

Division

Division is based on dividing a given number into parts. The simplest problem involves dividing a number into equal parts. For example, a pack of 20 pencils is to be divided among 10 children. You would have to divide 20 by 10. In this example, each child would receive 2 pencils.

The symbol for division is $\div$ or $/$. The equation above is written as $20 \div 10 = 2$, or $20 / 10 = 2$. This means "20 divided by 10 is equal to 2." Division can be explained as the following: for any whole numbers a and b, where b is not equal to zero, $a \div b = c$ if and only if $a = b \times c$. This means, division can be thought of as a multiplication problem with a missing part. For instance, calculating $20 \div 10$ is the same as asking the following: "If there are 20 items in total with 10 in each group, how many are in each group?" Therefore, 20 is equal to ten times what value? This question is the same as asking, "If there are 20 items in total with 2 in each group, how many groups are there?" The answer to each question is 2.

In a division problem, a is known as the **dividend**, b is the **divisor**, and c is the **quotient**. Zero cannot be divided into parts. Therefore, for any nonzero whole number a, $0 \div a = 0$. Also, division by zero is undefined. Dividing an amount into zero parts is not possible.

Harder division involves dividing a number into equal parts, but having some left over. An example is dividing a pack of 20 pencils among 8 friends so that each friend receives the same number of pencils. In this setting, each friend receives 2 pencils. There are 4 pencils leftover. 20 is the dividend, 8 is the divisor, 2 is the quotient, and 4 is known as the **remainder**. Within this type of division problem, for whole numbers a, b, c, and d, $a \div b = c$ with a remainder of d. This is true if and only if $a = (b \times c) + d$. When calculating $a \div b$, if there is no remainder, a is said to be *divisible* by b. **Even numbers** are all divisible by the number 2. **Odd numbers** are not divisible by 2. An odd number of items cannot be paired up into groups of 2 without having one item leftover.

Dividing a number by a single digit or two digits can be turned into repeated subtraction problems. An area model can be used throughout the problem that represents multiples of the divisor. For example, the answer to $8580 \div 55$ can be found by subtracting 55 from 8580 one at a time and counting the total number of subtractions necessary.

However, a simpler process involves using larger multiples of 55. First, $100 \times 55 = 5{,}500$ is subtracted from 8,580, and 3,080 is leftover. Next, $50 \times 55 = 2{,}750$ is subtracted from 3,080 to obtain380. $5 \times 55 = 275$ is subtracted from 330 to obtain 55, and finally, $1 \times 55 = 55$ is subtracted from 55 to obtain zero. Therefore, there is no remainder, and the answer is $100 + 50 + 5 + 1 = 156$. Here is a picture of the area model and the repeated subtraction process:

If you want to check the answer of a division problem, multiply the answer times the divisor. This will help you check to see if the dividend is obtained. If there is a remainder, the same process is done, but the remainder is added on at the end to try to match the dividend. In the previous example, $156 \times 64 = 9984$ would be the checking procedure. Dividing decimals involves the same repeated subtraction process. The only difference would be that the subtractions would involve numbers that include values in the decimal places. Lining up decimal places is crucial in this type of problem.

Using Operations in Math and Real-World Problems

Addition and subtraction are "inverse operations." Adding a number and then subtracting the same number will cancel each other out. This results in the original number, and vice versa. For example, $8 + 7 - 7 = 8$ and $137 - 100 + 100 = 137$.

Multiplication and division are also inverse operations. So, multiplying by a number and then dividing by the same number results in the original number. For example, $8 \times 2 \div 2 = 8$ and $12 \div 4 \times 4 = 12$. Inverse operations are used to work backwards to solve problems. In the case that 7 and a number add to 18, the inverse operation of subtraction is used to find the unknown value ($18 - 7 = 11$). If a school's entire 4th grade was divided evenly into 3 classes each with 22 students, the inverse operation of multiplication is used to determine the total students in the grade ($22 \times 3 = 66$). More scenarios involving inverse operations are listed in the tables below.

Word problems take concepts you learned in the classroom and turn them into real-life situations. Some parts of the problem are known and at least one part is unknown. There are three types of instances in which something can be unknown: the starting point, the change, or the final result. These can all be missing from the information they give you.

For an addition problem, the change is the quantity of a new amount added to the starting point.

For a subtraction problem, the change is the quantity taken away from the starting point.

Regarding addition, the given equation is $3 + 7 = 10$.

The number 3 is the starting point. 7 is the change, and 10 is the result from adding a new amount to the starting point. Different word problems can arise from this same equation, depending on which value is the unknown. For example, here are three problems:

- If a boy had 3 pencils and was given 7 more, how many would he have in total?

- If a boy had 3 pencils and a girl gave him more so that he had 10 in total, how many were given to him?

- A boy was given 7 pencils so that he had 10 in total. How many did he start with?

All three problems involve the same equation. Finding out which part of the equation is missing is the key to solving each word problem. The missing answers would be 10, 7, and 3.

In terms of subtraction, the same three scenarios can occur. The given equation is $6 - 4 = 2$.

The number 6 is the starting point. 4 is the change, and 2 is the new amount that is the result from taking away an amount from the starting point. Again, different types of word problems can arise from this equation. For example, here are three possible problems:

- If a girl had 6 quarters and 2 were taken away, how many would be left over?

- If a girl had 6 quarters, purchased a pencil, and had 2 quarters left over, how many did she pay with?

- If a girl paid for a pencil with 4 quarters and had 2 quarters left over, how many did she have to start with?

The three question types follow the structure of the addition word problems. Finding out whether the starting point, the change, or the final result is missing is the goal in solving the problem. The missing answers would be 2, 4, and 6.

The three addition problems and the three subtraction word problems can be solved by using a picture, a number line, or an algebraic equation. If an equation is used, a question mark can be used to show the number we don't know. For example, $6 - 4 =?$ can be written to show that the missing value is the result. Using equation form shows us what part of the addition or subtraction problem is missing.

Key words within a multiplication problem involve *times, product, doubled*, and *tripled*. Key words within a division problem involve *split, quotient, divided, shared, groups*, and *half*. Like addition and subtraction, multiplication and division problems also have three different types of missing values.

Multiplication consists of a certain number of groups, with the same number of items within each group, and the total amount within all groups. Therefore, each one of these amounts can be the missing value.

For example, the given equation is $5 \times 3 = 15$.

5 and 3 are interchangeable, so either amount can be the number of groups or the number of items within each group. 15 is the total number of items. Again, different types of word problems can arise from this equation. For example, here are three problems:

- If a classroom is serving 5 different types of apples for lunch and has 3 apples of each type, how many total apples are there to give to the students?

- If a classroom has 15 apples with 5 different types, how many of each type are there?

- If a classroom has 15 apples with 3 of each type, how many types are there to choose from?

Each question involves using the same equation to solve. It is important to decide which part of the equation is the missing value. The answers to the problems are 15, 3, and 5.

Similar to multiplication, division problems involve a total amount, a number of groups having the same amount, and a number of items within each group. The difference between multiplication and division is that the starting point is the total amount. It then gets divided into equal amounts.

For example, the equation is $15 \div 5 = 3$.

15 is the total number of items, which is being divided into 5 different groups. In order to do so, 3 items go into each group. Also, 5 and 3 are interchangeable. So, the 15 items could be divided into 3 groups of 5 items each. Therefore, different types of word problems can arise from this equation. For example, here are three types of problems:

- A boy needs 48 pieces of chalk. If there are 8 pieces in each box, how many boxes should he buy?

- A boy has 48 pieces of chalk. If each box has 6 pieces in it, how many boxes did he buy?

- A boy has partitioned all of his chalk into 8 piles, with 6 pieces in each pile. How many pieces does he have in total?

Each one of these questions involves the same equation. The third question can easily utilize the multiplication equation $8 \times 6 = ?$ instead of division. The answers are 6, 8, and 48.

Adding and Subtracting Positive and Negative Numbers

Some problems require adding positive and negative numbers or subtracting positive and negative numbers. Adding a negative number to a positive one can be thought of a reducing or subtracting from the positive number, and the result should be less than the positive number. For example, adding 8 and -3 is the same is subtracting 3 from 8; the result is 5. This can be visualized by imagining that the positive number (8) represents 8 apples that a student has in her basket. The negative number (-3) indicates the number of apples she is in debt or owes to her friend. In order to pay off her debt and "settle the score," she essentially is in possession of three fewer apples than in her basket (8 − 3 = 5), so she actually has five apples that are hers to keep. Should the negative addend be of higher magnitude than the positive addend (for example -9 + 3), the result will be negative, but "less negative" or closer to zero than the large negative number. This is because adding a positive value, even if relatively smaller, to a negative value, reduces the magnitude of the negative in the total. Considering the apple example again, if the girl owed 9 apples to her friend (-9) but she picked 3 (+3) off a tree and gave them to her friend, she now would only owe him six apples (-6), which reduced her debt burden (her negative number of apples) by three.

Subtracting positive and negative numbers works the same way with one key distinction: subtracting a negative number from a negative number yields a "less negative" or more positive result because again, this can be considered as removing or alleviating some debt. For example, if the student with the apples owed 5 apples to her friend, she essentially has -5 applies. If her mom gives that friend 10 apples on behalf of the girl, she now has removed the need to pay back the 5 apples and surpassed neutral (no net apples owed) and now her friend owes *her* five apples (+5). Stated mathematically -5 + -10 = +5.

Operations with Fractions, Decimals, and Percentages

Fractions
Fractions are a vital part of mathematics, and their understanding tends to be extremely challenging for students. Too often, steps are learned without understanding why they are being performed. It is important for teachers to make the concept of fractions less abstract and more tangible by providing concrete examples in the classroom. With this solid foundation and a lot of practice, learning will be easier, and success with fractions in later math classes will occur.

A **fraction** is a part of something that is whole. Items such as apples can be cut into parts to help visualize fractions. If an apple is cut into 2 equal parts, each part represents ½ of the apple. If each half is cut into two parts, the apple now is cut into quarters. Each piece now represents ¼ of the apple. In this example, each part is equal because they all have the same size. Geometric shapes, such as circles and squares, can also be utilized in the classroom to help visualize the idea of fractions. For example, a circle can be drawn on the board and divided into 6 equal parts:

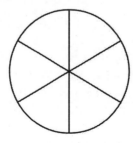

Shading can be used to represent parts of the circle that can be translated into fractions. The top of the fraction, the **numerator,** can represent how many segments are shaded. The bottom of the fraction, the **denominator,** can represent the number of segments that the circle is broken into. A pie is a good analogy to use in this example. If one piece of the circle is shaded, or one piece of pie is cut out, $^1/_6$ of the object is being referred to. An apple, a pie, or a circle can be utilized in order to compare simple fractions. For example, showing that ½ is larger than ¼ and that ¼ is smaller than $^1/_3$ can be accomplished through shading. A **unit fraction** is a fraction in which the numerator is 1, and the denominator is a positive whole number. It represents one part of a whole—one piece of pie.

Imagine that an apple pie has been baked for a holiday party, and the full pie has eight slices. After the party, there are five slices left. How could the amount of the pie that remains be expressed as a fraction? The numerator is 5 since there are 5 pieces left, and the denominator is 8 since there were eight total slices in the whole pie. Thus, expressed as a fraction, the leftover pie totals $\frac{5}{8}$ of the original amount.

Fractions come in three different varieties: proper fractions, improper fractions, and mixed numbers. **Proper fractions** have a numerator less than the denominator, such as $\frac{3}{8}$, but **improper fractions** have a numerator greater than the denominator, such as $\frac{15}{8}$. **Mixed numbers** combine a whole number with a proper fraction, such as $3\frac{1}{2}$. Any mixed number can be written as an improper fraction by multiplying the integer by the denominator, adding the product to the value of the numerator, and dividing the sum by the original denominator. For example, $3\frac{1}{2} = \frac{3 \times 2 + 1}{2} = \frac{7}{2}$. Whole numbers can also be converted into fractions by placing the whole number as the numerator and making the denominator 1. For example, $3 = \frac{3}{1}$.

The bar in a fraction represents division. Therefore $^6/_5$ is the same as $6 \div 5$. In order to rewrite it as a mixed number, division is performed to obtain $6 \div 5 = 1\ R1$. The remainder is then converted into fraction form. The actual remainder becomes the numerator of a fraction, and the divisor becomes the denominator. Therefore $1\ R1$ is written as $1\frac{1}{5}$, a mixed number. A mixed number can also decompose into the addition of a whole number and a fraction. For example,

$$1\frac{1}{5} = 1 + \frac{1}{5} \text{ and } 4\frac{5}{6} = 4 + \frac{1}{6} + \frac{1}{6} + \frac{1}{6} + \frac{1}{6} + \frac{1}{6}$$

Every fraction can be built from a combination of unit fractions.

One of the most fundamental concepts of fractions is their ability to be manipulated by multiplication or division. This is possible since $\frac{n}{n} = 1$ for any non-zero integer. As a result, multiplying or dividing by $\frac{n}{n}$ will not alter the original fraction since any number multiplied or divided by 1 doesn't change the value of that number. Fractions of the same value are known as equivalent fractions. For example, $\frac{2}{8}, \frac{25}{100}$, and $\frac{40}{160}$ are equivalent, as they all equal $\frac{1}{4}$.

Like fractions, or **equivalent fractions,** are the terms used to describe these fractions that are made up of different numbers but represent the same quantity. For example, the given fractions are $^4/_8$ and $^3/_6$. If a pie was cut into 8 pieces and 4 pieces were removed, half of the pie would remain. Also, if a pie was split into 6 pieces and 3 pieces were eaten, half of the pie would also remain. Therefore, both of the fractions represent half of a pie. These two fractions are referred to as like fractions. **Unlike fractions**

are fractions that are different and cannot be thought of as representing equal quantities. When working with fractions in mathematical expressions, like fractions should be simplified. Both $^4/_8$ and $^3/_6$ can be simplified into $^1/_2$.

Comparing fractions can be completed through the use of a number line. For example, if $^3/_5$ and $^6/_{10}$ need to be compared, each fraction should be plotted on a number line. To plot $^3/_5$, the area from 0 to 1 should be broken into 5 equal segments, and the fraction represents 3 of them. To plot $^6/_{10}$, the area from 0 to 1 should be broken into 10 equal segments and the fraction represents 6 of them.

It can be seen that $\dfrac{3}{5} = \dfrac{6}{10}$

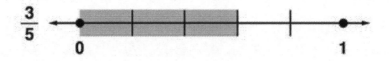

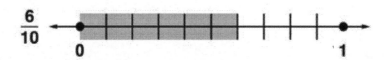

Like fractions are plotted at the same point on a number line. Unit fractions can also be used to compare fractions. For example, if it is known that

$$\frac{4}{5} > \frac{1}{2}$$

and

$$\frac{1}{2} > \frac{4}{10}$$

then it is also known that

$$\frac{4}{5} > \frac{4}{10}$$

Also, converting improper fractions to mixed numbers can be helpful in comparing fractions because the whole number portion of the number is more visible.

Adding and subtracting mixed numbers and fractions can be completed by decomposing fractions into a sum of whole numbers and unit fractions. For example, the given problem is

$$5\frac{3}{7} + 2\frac{1}{7}$$

Decomposing into

$$5 + \frac{1}{7} + \frac{1}{7} + \frac{1}{7} + 2 + \frac{1}{7}$$

This shows that the whole numbers can be added separately from the unit fractions. The answer is:

$$5 + 2 + \frac{1}{7} + \frac{1}{7} + \frac{1}{7} + \frac{1}{7} = 7 + \frac{4}{7} = 7\frac{4}{7}$$

Although many equivalent fractions exist, they are easier to compare and interpret when reduced or simplified. The numerator and denominator of a simple fraction will have no factors in common other than 1. When reducing or simplifying fractions, divide the numerator and denominator by the greatest common factor. A simple strategy is to divide the numerator and denominator by low numbers, like 2, 3, or 5 until arriving at a simple fraction, but the same thing could be achieved by determining the greatest common factor for both the numerator and denominator and dividing each by it. Using the first method is preferable when both the numerator and denominator are even, end in 5, or are obviously a multiple of another number. However, if no numbers seem to work, it will be necessary to factor the numerator and denominator to find the GCF. Let's look at examples:

1) Simplify the fraction $\frac{6}{8}$:

Dividing the numerator and denominator by 2 results in $\frac{3}{4}$, which is a simple fraction.

2) Simplify the fraction $\frac{12}{36}$:

Dividing the numerator and denominator by 2 leaves $\frac{6}{18}$. This isn't a simple fraction, as both the numerator and denominator have factors in common. Diving each by 3 results in $\frac{2}{6}$, but this can be further simplified by dividing by 2 to get $\frac{1}{3}$. This is the simplest fraction, as the numerator is 1. In cases like this, multiple division operations can be avoided by determining the greatest common factor between the numerator and denominator.

3) Simplify the fraction $\frac{18}{54}$ by dividing by the greatest common factor:

First, determine the factors for the numerator and denominator. The factors of 18 are 1, 2, 3, 6, 9, and 18. The factors of 54 are 1, 2, 3, 6, 9, 18, 27, and 54. Thus, the greatest common factor is 18. Dividing $\frac{18}{54}$ by 18 leaves $\frac{1}{3}$, which is the simplest fraction. This method takes slightly more work, but it definitively arrives at the simplest fraction.

Adding and Subtracting Fractions
Adding and subtracting fractions that have the same denominators involves adding or subtracting the numerators. The denominator will stay the same. Therefore, the decomposition process can be made simpler, and the fractions do not have to be broken into unit fractions.

For example, the given problem is:

$$4\frac{7}{8} - 2\frac{6}{8}$$

The answer is found by adding the answers to both

$$4 - 2 \text{ and } \frac{7}{8} - \frac{6}{8}$$

$$2 + \frac{1}{8} = 2\frac{1}{8}$$

A common mistake would be to add the denominators so that

$$\frac{1}{4} + \frac{1}{4} = \frac{1}{8} \text{ or } \frac{2}{8}$$

However, conceptually, it is known that two quarters make a half, so neither one of these are correct.

If two fractions have different denominators, equivalent fractions must be used to add or subtract them. The fractions must be converted into fractions that have common denominators. A **least common denominator** or the product of the two denominators can be used as the common denominator. For example, in the problem $\frac{5}{6} + \frac{2}{3}$, both 6, which is the least common denominator, and 18, which is the product of the denominators, can be used. In order to use 6, $\frac{2}{3}$ must be converted to sixths. A number line can be used to show the equivalent fraction is $\frac{4}{6}$. What happens is that $\frac{2}{3}$ is multiplied times a fractional form of 1 to obtain a denominator of 6. Hence, $\frac{2}{3} \times \frac{2}{2} = \frac{4}{6}$. Therefore, the problem is now $\frac{5}{6} + \frac{4}{6} = \frac{9}{6}$, which can be simplified into $\frac{3}{2}$. In order to use 18, both fractions must be converted into having 18 as their denominator. $\frac{5}{6}$ would have to be multiplied times $\frac{3}{3}$, and $\frac{2}{3}$ would need to be multiplied times $\frac{6}{6}$. The addition problem would be $\frac{15}{18} + \frac{12}{18} = \frac{27}{18}$, which reduces into $\frac{3}{2}$.

It is always possible to find a common denominator by multiplying the denominators. However, when the denominators are large numbers, this method is unwieldy, especially if the answer must be provided in its simplest form. Thus, it's beneficial to find the **least common denominator** of the fractions—the least common denominator is incidentally also the **least common multiple**.

Once equivalent fractions have been found with common denominators, simply add or subtract the numerators to arrive at the answer:

1) $\frac{1}{2} + \frac{3}{4} = \frac{2}{4} + \frac{3}{4} = \frac{5}{4}$

2) $\frac{3}{12} + \frac{11}{20} = \frac{15}{60} + \frac{33}{60} = \frac{48}{60} = \frac{4}{5}$

3) $\frac{7}{9} - \frac{4}{15} = \frac{35}{45} - \frac{12}{45} = \frac{23}{45}$

4) $\frac{5}{6} - \frac{7}{18} = \frac{15}{18} - \frac{7}{18} = \frac{8}{18} = \frac{4}{9}$

Multiplying and Dividing Fractions
Of the four basic operations that can be performed on fractions, the one which involves the least amount of work is multiplication. To multiply two fractions, simply multiply the numerators, multiply the denominators, and place the products as a fraction. Whole numbers and mixed numbers can also be expressed as a fraction, as described above, to multiply with a fraction.

Because multiplication is commutative, multiplying a fraction times a whole number is the same as multiplying a whole number times a fraction. The problem involves adding a fraction a specific number of times. The problem $3 \times \frac{1}{4}$ can be translated into adding the unit fraction 3 times: $\frac{1}{4} + \frac{1}{4} + \frac{1}{4} = \frac{3}{4}$. In the problem $4 \times \frac{2}{5}$, the fraction can be decomposed into $\frac{1}{5} + \frac{1}{5}$ and then added 4 times to obtain $\frac{8}{5}$. Also, both of these answers can be found by just multiplying the whole number times the numerator of the fraction being multiplied.

The whole numbers can be written in fraction form as:

$$\frac{3}{1} \times \frac{1}{4} = \frac{3}{4}$$

$$\frac{4}{1} \times \frac{2}{5} = \frac{8}{5}$$

Multiplying a fraction times a fraction involves multiplying the numerators together separately and the denominators together separately. For example,

$$\frac{3}{8} \times \frac{2}{3} = \frac{3 \times 2}{8 \times 3} = \frac{6}{24}$$

This can then be reduced to $^1/_4$.

Dividing a fraction by a fraction is actually a multiplication problem. It involves flipping the divisor and then multiplying normally. For example,

$$\frac{22}{5} \div \frac{1}{2} = \frac{22}{5} \times \frac{2}{1} = \frac{44}{5}$$

The same procedure can be implemented for division problems involving fractions and whole numbers. The whole number can be rewritten as a fraction over a denominator of 1, and then division can be completed.

A common denominator approach can also be used in dividing fractions. Considering the same problem, $\frac{22}{5} \div \frac{1}{2}$, a common denominator between the two fractions is 10. $\frac{22}{5}$ would be rewritten as $\frac{22}{5} \times \frac{2}{2} = \frac{44}{10}$, and $\frac{1}{2}$ would be rewritten as $\frac{1}{2} \times \frac{5}{5} = \frac{5}{10}$. Dividing both numbers straight across results in:

$$\frac{44}{10} \div \frac{5}{10} = \frac{^{44}/_5}{^{10}/_{10}} = \frac{^{44}/_5}{1} = {^{44}/_5}$$

Many real-world problems will involve the use of fractions. Key words include actual fraction values, such as half, quarter, third, fourth, etc. The best approach to solving word problems involving fractions is to draw a picture or diagram that represents the scenario being discussed, while deciding which type of operation is necessary in order to solve the problem. A phrase such as "one fourth of 60 pounds of coal" creates a scenario in which multiplication should be used, and the mathematical form of the phrase is $\frac{1}{4} \times 60$.

<u>Decimals</u>

The **decimal system** is a way of writing out numbers that uses ten different numerals: 0, 1, 2, 3, 4, 5, 6, 7, 8, and 9. This is also called a "base ten" or "base 10" system. Other bases are also used. For example, computers work with a base of 2. This means they only use the numerals 0 and 1.

The **decimal place** denotes how far to the right of the decimal point a numeral is. The first digit to the right of the decimal point is in the *tenths* place. The next is the **hundredths**. The third is the **thousandths**.

So, 3.142 has a 1 in the tenths place, a 4 in the hundredths place, and a 2 in the thousandths place.

The **decimal point** is a period used to separate the **ones** place from the **tenths** place when writing out a number as a decimal.

A **decimal number** is a number written out with a decimal point instead of as a fraction, for example, 1.25 instead of $\frac{5}{4}$. Depending on the situation, it can sometimes be easier to work with fractions and sometimes easier to work with decimal numbers.

A decimal number is **terminating** if it stops at some point. It is called **repeating** if it never stops but repeats a pattern over and over. It is important to note that every rational number can be written as a terminating decimal or as a repeating decimal.

Addition with Decimals

To add decimal numbers, each number in columns needs to be lined up by the decimal point. For each number being added, the zeros to the right of the last number need to be filled in so that each of the numbers has the same number of places to the right of the decimal. Then, the columns can be added together. Here is an example of 2.45 + 1.3 + 8.891 written in column form:

$$\begin{array}{r} 2.450 \\ 1.300 \\ + 8.891 \\ \hline \end{array}$$

Zeros have been added in the columns so that each number has the same number of places to the right of the decimal.

Added together, the correct answer is 12.641:

$$\begin{array}{r} 2.450 \\ 1.300 \\ + 8.891 \\ \hline 12.641 \end{array}$$

Subtraction with Decimals

Subtracting decimal numbers is the same process as adding decimals. Here is 7.89 − 4.235 written in column form:

$$\begin{array}{r} 7.890 \\ - 4.235 \\ \hline 3.655 \end{array}$$

A zero has been added in the column so that each number has the same number of places to the right of the decimal.

Multiplication with Decimals
Decimals can be multiplied as if there were no decimal points in the problem. For example, 0.5 x 1.25 can be rewritten and multiplied as 5 x 125, which equals 625.

The final answer will have the same number of decimal *points* as the total number of decimal *places* in the problem. The first number has one decimal place, and the second number has two decimal places. Therefore, the final answer will contain three decimal places:

$$0.5 \text{ x } 1.25 = 0.625$$

Division with Decimals
Dividing a decimal by a whole number entails using long division first by ignoring the decimal point. Then, the decimal point is moved the number of places given in the problem.

For example, 6.8 ÷ 4 can be rewritten as 68 ÷ 4, which is 17. There is one non-zero integer to the right of the decimal point, so the final solution would have one decimal place to the right of the solution. In this case, the solution is 1.7.

Dividing a decimal by another decimal requires changing the divisor to a whole number by moving its decimal point. The decimal place of the dividend should be moved by the same number of places as the divisor. Then, the problem is the same as dividing a decimal by a whole number.

For example, 5.72 ÷ 1.1 has a divisor with one decimal point in the denominator. The expression can be rewritten as 57.2 ÷ 11 by moving each number one decimal place to the right to eliminate the decimal. The long division can be completed as 572 ÷ 11 with a result of 52. Since there is one non-zero integer to the right of the decimal point in the problem, the final solution is 5.2.

In another example, 8 ÷ 0.16 has a divisor with two decimal points in the denominator. The expression can be rewritten as 800 ÷ 16 by moving each number two decimal places to the right to eliminate the decimal in the divisor. The long division can be completed with a result of 50.

Percentages
Think of percentages as fractions with a denominator of 100. In fact, percentage means "per hundred." Problems often require converting numbers from percentages, fractions, and decimals.

The basic percent equation is the following:

$$\frac{is}{of} = \frac{\%}{100}$$

The placement of numbers in the equation depends on what the question asks.

Example 1
Find 40% of 80.

Basically, the problem is asking, "What is 40% of 80?" The 40% is the percent, and 80 is the number to find the percent "of." The equation is:

$$\frac{x}{80} = \frac{40}{100}$$

Solving the equation by cross-multiplication, the problem becomes 100x = 80(40). Solving for x gives the answer: x = 32.

Example 2
What percent of 100 is 20?

The 20 fills in the "is" portion, while 100 fills in the "of." The question asks for the percent, so that will be x, the unknown. The following equation is set up:

$$\frac{20}{100} = \frac{x}{100}$$

Cross-multiplying yields the equation 100x = 20(100). Solving for x gives the answer of 20%.

Example 3
30% of what number is 30?

The following equation uses the clues and numbers in the problem:

$$\frac{30}{x} = \frac{30}{100}$$

Cross-multiplying results in the equation 30(100) = 30x. Solving for x gives the answer x = 100.

Conversions
Decimals and Percentages
Since a percentage is based on "per hundred," decimals and percentages can be converted by multiplying or dividing by 100. Practically speaking, this always amounts to moving the decimal point two places to the right or left, depending on the conversion. To convert a percentage to a decimal, move the decimal point two places to the left and remove the % sign. To convert a decimal to a percentage, move the decimal point two places to the right and add a "%" sign. Here are some examples:

    65% = 0.65
    0.33 = 33%
    0.215 = 21.5%
    99.99% = 0.9999
    500% = 5.00
    7.55 = 755%

Fractions and Percentages

Remember that a percentage is a number per one hundred. So a percentage can be converted to a fraction by making the number in the percentage the numerator and putting 100 as the denominator:

$$43\% = \frac{43}{100}$$

$$97\% = \frac{97}{100}$$

Note that the percent symbol (%) kind of looks like a 0, a 1, and another 0. So think of a percentage like 54% as 54 over 100.

To convert a fraction to a percent, follow the same logic. If the fraction happens to have 100 in the denominator, you're in luck. Just take the numerator and add a percent symbol:

$$\frac{28}{100} = 28\%$$

Otherwise, divide the numerator by the denominator to get a decimal:

$$\frac{9}{12} = 0.75$$

Then convert the decimal to a percentage:

$$0.75 = 75\%$$

Another option is to make the denominator equal to 100. Be sure to multiply the numerator by the same number as the denominator. For example:

$$\frac{3}{20} \times \frac{5}{5} = \frac{15}{100}$$

$$\frac{15}{100} = 15\%$$

Changing Fractions to Decimals

To change a fraction into a decimal, divide the denominator into the numerator until there are no remainders. There may be repeating decimals, so rounding is often acceptable. A straight line above the repeating portion denotes that the decimal repeats.

<u>Example</u>
Express 4/5 as a decimal.

Set up the division problem.

$$5\overline{)4}$$

5 does not go into 4, so place the decimal and add a zero.

$$5\overline{)4.0}$$

5 goes into 40 eight times. There is no remainder.

$$\begin{array}{r} 0\,.\,8 \\ 5\overline{)4\,.\,0} \\ -\,4\,.\,0 \\ \hline 0 \end{array}$$

The solution is 0.8.

Example
Express 33 1/3 as a decimal.

Since the whole portion of the number is known, set it aside to calculate the decimal from the fraction portion.

Set up the division problem.

$$3\overline{)1}$$

3 does not go into 1, so place the decimal and add zeros. 3 goes into 10 three times.

$$\begin{array}{r} 0\,.\,3 \\ 3\overline{)1\,.\,0} \end{array}$$

This will repeat with a remainder of 1.

$$\begin{array}{r} 0\,.\,3\,3\,3 \\ 3\overline{)1\,.\,0\,0\,0} \\ -\,9 \\ \hline 1\,0 \\ -\,9 \\ \hline 1\,0 \end{array}$$

So, we will place a line over the 3 to denote the repetition. The solution is written $0.\overline{3}$.

Changing Decimals to Fractions
To change decimals to fractions, place the decimal portion of the number, the numerator, over the respective place value, the denominator, then reduce, if possible.

Example: Express 0.25 as a fraction.

This is read as twenty-five hundredths, so put 25 over 100. Then reduce to find the solution.

$$\frac{25}{100} = \frac{1}{4}$$

Example: Express 0.455 as a fraction

This is read as four hundred fifty-five thousandths, so put 455 over 1000. Then reduce to find the solution.

$$\frac{455}{1000} = \frac{91}{200}$$

There are two types of problems that commonly involve percentages. The first is to calculate some percentage of a given quantity, where you convert the percentage to a decimal, and multiply the quantity by that decimal. Secondly, you are given a quantity and told it is a fixed percent of an unknown quantity. In this case, convert to a decimal, then divide the given quantity by that decimal.

Example: What is 30% of 760?

Convert the percent into a useable number. "Of" means to multiply.

$$30\% = 0.30$$

Set up the problem based on the givens, and solve.

$$0.30 \times 760 = 228$$

Example: 8.4 is 20% of what number?

Convert the percent into a useable number.

$$20\% = 0.20$$

The given number is a percent of the answer needed, so divide the given number by this decimal rather than multiplying it.

$$\frac{8.4}{0.20} = 42$$

Solving Practical Math Problems

Word problems, or story problems, are math problems that have a real-world context. In word problems, multiple quantities are often provided with a request to find some kind of relation between them. This often will mean that one variable (the dependent variable whose value needs to be found) can be written as a function of another variable (the independent variable whose value can be figured from the given information). The usual procedure for solving these problems is to start by giving each quantity in the problem a variable, and then figuring the relationship between these variables.

For example, suppose a car gets 25 miles per gallon. How far will the car travel if it uses 2.4 gallons of fuel? In this case, y would be the distance the car has traveled in miles, and x would be the amount of fuel burned in gallons (2.4). Then the relationship between these variables can be written as an algebraic equation, $y = 25x$. In this case, the equation is $y = 25 \times 2.4 = 60$, so the car has traveled 60 miles.

Translating Verbal Relationships into Algebraic Equations or Expressions
When attempting to solve a math problem, it's important to apply the correct algorithm. It is much more difficult to determine what algorithm is necessary when solving word problems, because the

necessary operations and equations are typically not provided. In these instances, the test taker must translate the words in the problem into true mathematical statements that can be solved. The following are examples:

Symbol	Phrase
+	Added to; increased by; sum of; more than
−	Decreased by; difference between; less than; take away
×	Multiplied by; 3(4,5...) times as large; product of
÷	Divided by; quotient of; half (third, etc.) of
=	Is; the same as; results in; as much as; equal to
x,t,n, etc.	A number; unknown quantity; value of; variable

Addition and subtraction are **inverse operations**. Adding a number and then subtracting the same number will cancel each other out, resulting in the original number, and vice versa. For example, $8 + 7 - 7 = 8$ and $137 - 100 + 100 = 137$. Similarly, multiplication and division are inverse operations. Therefore, multiplying by a number and then dividing by the same number results in the original number, and vice versa. For example, $8 \times 2 \div 2 = 8$ and $12 \div 4 \times 4 = 12$. Inverse operations are used to work backwards to solve problems. In the case that 7 and a number add to 18, the inverse operation of subtraction is used to find the unknown value ($18 - 7 = 11$). If a school's entire 4th grade was divided evenly into 3 classes each with 22 students, the inverse operation of multiplication is used to determine the total students in the grade ($22 \times 3 = 66$). Additional scenarios involving inverse operations are included in the tables below.

There are a variety of real-world situations in which one or more of the operators is used to solve a problem. The tables below display the most common scenarios.

Addition & Subtraction

	Unknown Result	Unknown Change	Unknown Start
Adding to	5 students were in class. 4 more students arrived. How many students are in class? $5+4=?$	8 students were in class. More students arrived late. There are now 18 students in class. How many students arrived late? $8+?=18$ Solved by inverse operations $18-8=?$	Some students were in class early. 11 more students arrived. There are now 17 students in class. How many students were in class early? $?+11=17$ Solved by inverse operations $17-11=?$
Taking from	15 students were in class. 5 students left class. How many students are in class now? $15-5=?$	12 students were in class. Some students left class. There are now 8 students in class. How many students left class? $12-?=8$ Solved by inverse operations $8+?=12 \rightarrow 12-8=?$	Some students were in class. 3 students left class. Then there were 13 students in class. How many students were in class before? $?-3=13$ Solved by inverse operations $13+3=?$

	Unknown Total	Unknown Addends (Both)	Unknown Addends (One)
Putting together/ taking apart	The homework assignment is 10 addition problems and 8 subtraction problems. How many problems are in the homework assignment? $10+8=?$	Bobby has $9. How much can Bobby spend on candy and how much can Bobby spend on toys? $9=?+?$	Bobby has 12 pairs of pants. 5 pairs of pants are shorts, and the rest are long. How many pairs of long pants does he have? $12=5+?$ Solved by inverse operations $12-5=?$

	Unknown Difference	**Unknown Larger Value**	**Unknown Smaller Value**
Comparing	Bobby has 5 toys. Tommy has 8 toys. How many more toys does Tommy have than Bobby? $5 + ? = 8$ Solved by inverse operations $8 - 5 = ?$ Bobby has \$6. Tommy has \$10. How many fewer dollars does Bobby have than Tommy? $10 - 6 = ?$	Tommy has 2 more toys than Bobby. Bobby has 4 toys. How many toys does Tommy have? $2 + 4 = ?$ Bobby has 3 fewer dollars than Tommy. Bobby has \$8. How many dollars does Tommy have? $? - 3 = 8$ Solved by inverse operations $8 + 3 = ?$	Tommy has 6 more toys than Bobby. Tommy has 10 toys. How many toys does Bobby have? $? + 6 = 10$ Solved by inverse operations $10 - 6 = ?$ Bobby has \$5 less than Tommy. Tommy has \$9. How many dollars does Bobby have? $9 - 5 = ?$

Multiplication and Division

	Unknown Product	**Unknown Group Size**	**Unknown Number of Groups**
Equal groups	There are 5 students, and each student has 4 pieces of candy. How many pieces of candy are there in all? $5 \times 4 = ?$	14 pieces of candy are shared equally by 7 students. How many pieces of candy does each student have? $7 \times ? = 14$ Solved by inverse operations $14 \div 7 = ?$	If 18 pieces of candy are to be given out 3 to each student, how many students will get candy? $? \times 3 = 18$ Solved by inverse operations $18 \div 3 = ?$

	Unknown Product	**Unknown Factor**	**Unknown Factor**
Arrays	There are 5 rows of students with 3 students in each row. How many students are there? $5 \times 3 = ?$	If 16 students are arranged into 4 equal rows, how many students will be in each row? $4 \times ? = 16$ Solved by inverse operations $16 \div 4 = ?$	If 24 students are arranged into an array with 6 columns, how many rows are there? $? \times 6 = 24$ Solved by inverse operations $24 \div 6 = ?$

	Larger Unknown	Smaller Unknown	Multiplier Unknown
Comparing	A small popcorn costs $1.50. A large popcorn costs 3 times as much as a small popcorn. How much does a large popcorn cost? $1.50 \times 3 =?$	A large soda costs $6 and that is 2 times as much as a small soda costs. How much does a small soda cost? $2 \times ? = 6$ Solved by inverse operations $6 \div 2 =?$	A large pretzel costs $3 and a small pretzel costs $2. How many times as much does the large pretzel cost as the small pretzel? $? \times 2 = 3$ Solved by inverse operations $3 \div 2 =?$

<u>Modeling and Solving Word Problems</u>

Word problems can appear daunting, but don't let the wording intimidate you. No matter the scenario or specifics, the key to answering them is to translate the words into a math problem. Always keep in mind what the question is asking and what operations could lead to that answer.

Some word problems require more than just one simple equation to be written and solved. Consider the following situations and the linear equations used to model them.

Suppose Margaret is 2 miles to the east of John at noon. Margaret walks to the east at 3 miles per hour. How far apart will they be at 3 p.m.? To solve this, x would represent the time in hours past noon, and y would represent the distance between Margaret and John. Now, noon corresponds to the equation where x is 0, so the y intercept is going to be 2. It's also known that the slope will be the rate at which the distance is changing, which is 3 miles per hour. This means that the slope will be 3 (be careful at this point: if units were used, other than miles and hours, for x and y variables, a conversion of the given information to the appropriate units would be required first). The simplest way to write an equation given the y-intercept, and the slope is the Slope-Intercept form, is $y = mx + b$. Recall that m here is the slope and b is the y intercept. So, $m = 3$ and $b = 2$. Therefore, the equation will be $y = 3x + 2$. The word problem asks how far to the east Margaret will be from John at 3 p.m., which means when x is 3. So, substitute $x = 3$ into this equation to obtain $y = 3 \cdot 3 + 2 = 9 + 2 = 11$. Therefore, she will be 11 miles to the east of him at 3 p.m.

For another example, suppose that a box with 4 cans in it weighs 6 lbs., while a box with 8 cans in it weighs 12 lbs. Find out how much a single can weighs. To do this, let x denote the number of cans in the box, and y denote the weight of the box with the cans in lbs. This line touches two pairs: $(4, 6)$ and $(8, 12)$. A formula for this relation could be written using the two-point form, with $x_1 = 4, y_1 = 6, x_2 = 8, y_2 = 12$. This would yield $\frac{y-6}{x-4} = \frac{12-6}{8-4}$, or $\frac{y-6}{x-4} = \frac{6}{4} = \frac{3}{2}$. However, only the slope is needed to solve this problem, since the slope will be the weight of a single can. From the computation, the slope is $\frac{3}{2}$. Therefore, each can weighs $\frac{3}{2}$ lb.

Solving Simple Algebraic Problems

Linear equations and **linear inequalities** are both comparisons of two algebraic expressions. However, unlike equations in which the expressions are equal, linear inequalities compare expressions that may be unequal. Linear equations typically have one value for the variable that makes the statement true. Linear inequalities generally have an infinite number of values that make the statement true.

When solving a linear equation, the desired result requires determining a numerical value for the unknown **variable**. If given a linear equation involving addition, subtraction, multiplication, or division, working backwards isolates the variable. Addition and subtraction are inverse operations, as are multiplication and division. Therefore, they can be used to cancel each other out.

Since variables are the letters that represent an unknown number, you must solve for that unknown number in single variable problems. The main thing to remember is that you can do anything to one side of an equation as long as you do it to the other.

The first steps to solving linear equations are distributing, if necessary, and combining any like terms on the same side of the equation. Sides of an equation are separated by an **equal sign**. Next, the equation is manipulated to show the variable on one side. Again, whatever is done to one side of the equation must be done to the other side of the equation to remain equal. Inverse operations are then used to isolate the variable and undo the order of operations backwards. Addition and subtraction are undone, then multiplication and division are undone.

For example, solve $4(t - 2) + 2t - 4 = 2(9 - 2t)$

Distributing: $4t - 8 + 2t - 4 = 18 - 4t$

Combining like terms: $6t - 12 = 18 - 4t$

Adding $4t$ to each side to move the variable: $10t - 12 = 18$

Adding 12 to each side to isolate the variable: $10t = 30$

Dividing each side by 10 to isolate the variable: $t = 3$

The answer can be checked by substituting the value for the variable into the original equation, ensuring that both sides calculate to be equal.

Linear inequalities express the relationship between unequal values. More specifically, they describe in what way the values are unequal. A value can be greater than (>), less than (<), greater than or equal to (≥), or less than or equal to (≤) another value. $5x + 40 > 65$ is read as *five times a number added to forty is greater than sixty-five.*

When solving a linear inequality, the solution is the set of all numbers that make the statement true. The inequality $x + 2 \geq 6$ has a solution set of 4 and every number greater than 4 (4.01; 5; 12; 107; etc.). Adding 2 to 4 or any number greater than 4 results in a value that is greater than or equal to 6. Therefore, $x \geq 4$ is the solution set.

To algebraically solve a linear inequality, follow the same steps as those for solving a linear equation. The inequality symbol stays the same for all operations except when multiplying or dividing by a negative number. If multiplying or dividing by a negative number while solving an inequality, the relationship reverses (the sign flips). In other words, > switches to < and vice versa. Multiplying or dividing by a positive number does not change the relationship, so the sign stays the same.

An example is shown below.

Solve $-2x - 8 \leq 22$

Add 8 to both sides: $-2x \leq 30$

Divide both sides by -2: $x \geq -15$

Although linear equations generally have one solution, this is not always the case. If there is no value for the variable that makes the statement true, there is no solution to the equation. Consider the equation $x + 3 = x - 1$. There is no value for x in which adding 3 to the value produces the same result as subtracting one from the value. Conversely, if any value for the variable makes a true statement, the equation has an infinite number of solutions. Consider the equation $3x + 6 = 3(x + 2)$. Any number substituted for x will result in a true statement (both sides of the equation are equal).

By manipulating equations like the two above, the variable of the equation will cancel out completely. If the remaining constants express a true statement (ex. $6 = 6$), then all real numbers are solutions to the equation. If the constants left express a false statement (ex. $3 = -1$), then no solution exists for the equation.

When solving radical and rational equations, extraneous solutions must be accounted for when finding the answers. For example, the equation $\frac{x}{x-5} = \frac{3x}{x+3}$ has two values that create a 0 denominator: $x \neq 5, -3$. When solving for x, these values must be considered because they cannot be solutions. In the given equation, solving for x can be done using cross-multiplication, yielding the equation $x(x + 3) = 3x(x - 5)$. Distributing results in the quadratic equation yields $x^2 + 3x = 3x^2 - 15x$; therefore, all terms must be moved to one side of the equals sign. This results in $2x^2 - 18x = 0$, which in factored form is $2x(x - 9) = 0$. Setting each factor equal to zero, the apparent solutions are $x = 0$ and $x = 9$. These two solutions are neither 5 nor -3, so they are viable solutions. Neither 0 nor 9 create a 0 denominator in the original equation.

A similar process exists when solving radical equations. One must check to make sure the solutions are defined in the original equations. Solving an equation containing a square root involves isolating the root and then squaring both sides of the equals sign. Solving a cube root equation involves isolating the radical and then cubing both sides. In either case, the variable can then be solved for because there are no longer radicals in the equation.

Solving a linear inequality requires all values that make the statement true to be determined. For example, solving $3x - 7 \geq -13$ produces the solution $x \geq -2$. This means that -2 and any number greater than -2 produces a true statement. Solution sets for linear inequalities will often be displayed using a number line. If a value is included in the set ($\geq$ or $\leq$), a shaded dot is placed on that value and an arrow extending in the direction of the solutions. For a variable > or $\geq$ a number, the arrow will point right on a number line, the direction where the numbers increase. If a variable is < or $\leq$ a number, the arrow will point left on a number line, which is the direction where the numbers decrease. If the value is not included in the set (> or <), an open (unshaded) circle on that value is used with an arrow in the appropriate direction.

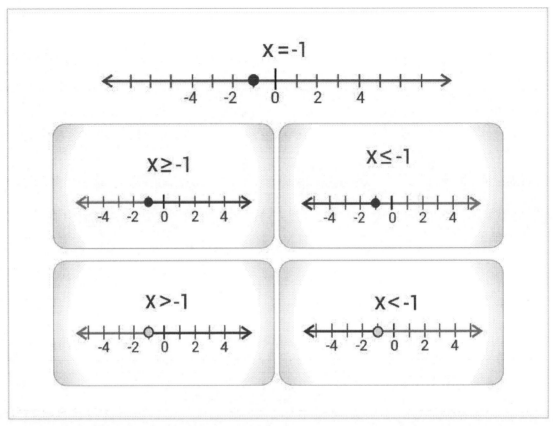

Similar to linear equations, a linear inequality may have a solution set consisting of all real numbers, or can contain no solution. When solved algebraically, a linear inequality in which the variable cancels out and results in a true statement (ex. $7 \geq 2$) has a solution set of all real numbers. A linear inequality in which the variable cancels out and results in a false statement (ex. $7 \leq 2$) has no solution.

Equations and inequalities in two variables represent a relationship. Jim owns a car wash and charges $40 per car. The rent for the facility is $350 per month. An equation can be written to relate the number of cars Jim cleans to the money he makes per month. Let x represent the number of cars and y represent the profit Jim makes each month from the car wash. The equation $y = 40x - 350$ can be used to show Jim's profit or loss. Since this equation has two variables, the coordinate plane can be used to show the relationship and predict profit or loss for Jim. The following graph shows that Jim must wash at least nine cars to pay the rent, where $x = 9$. Anything nine cars and above yield a profit shown in the value on the y-axis.

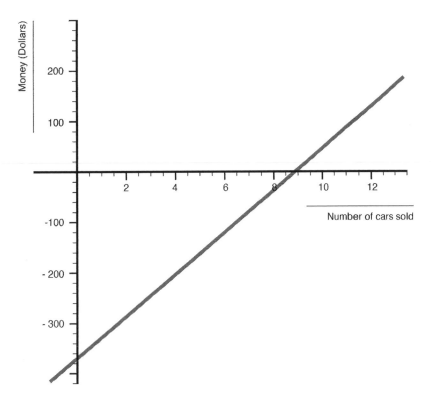

With a single equation in two variables, the solutions are limited only by the situation the equation represents. When two equations or inequalities are used, more constraints are added. For example, in a system of linear equations, there is often—although not always—only one answer. The point of intersection of two lines is the solution. For a system of inequalities, there are infinitely many answers.

The intersection of two solution sets gives the solution set of the system of inequalities. In the following graph, the darker shaded region is where two inequalities overlap. Any set of x and y found in that region satisfies both inequalities. The line with the positive slope is solid, meaning the values on that line are included in the solution. The line with the negative slope is dotted, so the coordinates on that line are not included.

Here's an example:

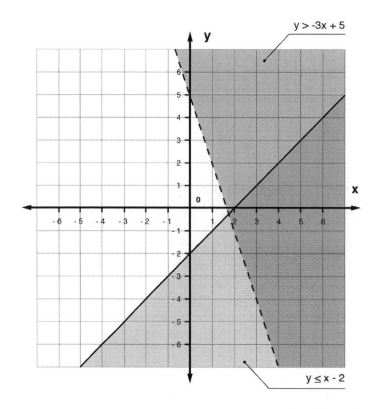

$y > -3x + 5$

$y \leq x - 2$

Formulas with two variables are equations used to represent a specific relationship. For example, the formula $d = rt$ represents the relationship between distance, rate, and time. If Bob travels at a rate of 35 miles per hour on his road trip from Westminster to Seneca, the formula $d = 35t$ can be used to represent his distance traveled in a specific length of time. Formulas can also be used to show different roles of the variables, transformed without any given numbers. Solving for r, the formula becomes $\frac{d}{t} = r$. The t is moved over by division so that *rate* is a function of distance and time.

The Problem-Solving Process and Determining If Enough Information Is Provided to Solve a Problem

Overall, the problem-solving process in mathematics involves a step-by-step procedure that one must follow when deciding what approach to take. First, one must understand the problem by deciding what is being sought, then if enough information is given, and what units are necessary in the solution. This is a crucial, but sometimes difficult step. It involves carefully reading the entire problem, identifying (perhaps even underlining) the facts or information that *is* known, and then deciphering the question words to determine what the problem is asking. In this way, math problems require students to be detectives, evaluating the "clues" or facts given in the problem, deciding what the problem is looking for, and evaluating whether sufficient information or "clues" are presented in the problem to solve the posed question.

In general, when solving word problems (also called story problems), it's important to understand what is being asked and to properly set up the initial equation. Always read the entire problem through, and then separate out what information is given in the statement. Decide what you are being asked to find and label each quantity with a variable or constant. Then write an equation to determine the unknown variable. Remember to label answers; sometimes knowing what the answers' units can help eliminate other possible solutions.

When trying to solve any word problem, look for a series of key words indicating addition, subtraction, multiplication, or division to help you determine how to set up the problem:

Addition: add, altogether, together, plus, increased by, more than, in all, sum, and total

Subtraction: minus, less than, difference, decreased by, fewer than, remain, and take away

Multiplication: *times*, *twice*, *of*, *double*, and *triple*

Division: divided by, cut up, half, quotient of, split, and shared equally

If a question asks to give words to a mathematical expression and says "equals," then an = sign must be included in the answer. Similarly, "less than or equal to" is expressed by the inequality symbol ≤, and "greater than or equal" to is expressed as ≥. Furthermore, "less than" is represented by <, and "greater than" is expressed by >.

These strategies are applicable to other question types. For example, calculating salary after deductions, balancing a checkbook, and calculating a dinner bill are common word problems similar to business planning. Just remember to use the correct operations. When a balance is increased, use addition. When a balance is decreased, use subtraction. Common sense and organization are your greatest assets when answering word problems.

For example, suppose the following word problem is encountered:

Walter's Coffee Shop sells a variety of drinks and breakfast treats.

Price List	
Hot Coffee	$2.00
Slow-Drip Iced Coffee	$3.00
Latte	$4.00
Muffin	$2.00
Crepe	$4.00
Egg Sandwich	$5.00

Costs	
Hot Coffee	$0.25
Slow-Drip Iced Coffee	$0.75
Latte	$1.00
Muffin	$1.00
Crepe	$2.00
Egg Sandwich	$3.00

Walter's utilities, rent, and labor costs him $500 per day. Today, Walter sold 200 hot coffees, 100 slow-drip iced coffees, 50 lattes, 75 muffins, 45 crepes, and 60 egg sandwiches. What was Walter's total profit today?

First, it is necessary to establish what is known (the "facts"), what one wants to know, (the question), how to determine the answer (the process), and if there is enough information to solve (sufficient "clues"). The problem clearly asks: "what was Walter's total profit today," so to accurately answer this type of question, the total cost of making his drinks and treats must be calculated, then the total revenue he earned from selling those products must be determined. After arriving at these two totals, the profit is measured found by deducting the total cost from the total revenue.

Now that the question and steps are identified, the provided facts are evaluated. Walter's costs for today:

Item	Quantity	Cost Per Unit	Total Cost
Hot Coffee	200	$0.25	$50
Slow-Drip Iced Coffee	100	$0.75	$75
Latte	50	$1.00	$50
Muffin	75	$1.00	$75
Crepe	45	$2.00	$90
Egg Sandwich	60	$3.00	$180
Utilities, rent, and labor			$500
Total Costs			$1,020

Walter's revenue for today:

Item	Quantity	Revenue Per Unit	Total Revenue
Hot Coffee	200	$2.00	$400
Slow-Drip Iced Coffee	100	$3.00	$300
Latte	50	$4.00	$200
Muffin	75	$2.00	$150
Crepe	45	$4.00	$180
Egg Sandwich	60	$5.00	$300
Total Revenue			$1,530

Walter's Profit = *Revenue – Costs* = $1,530 – $1,020 = $510

In this case, enough information was given in the problem to adequately solve it. If, however, the number of sandwiches and drinks were not provided, or Walter's cost per unit sold, insufficient information would prevent one from arriving at the answer.

Alternative Methods for Solving Mathematical Problems

When solving a math problem, once the question is identified and the clues are evaluated, the plan of action must be determined. In some cases, there might be many options. Therefore, one should begin with one approach and if the strategy does not fit, he or she should move on to another. In some cases, a combination of approaches can be used. A beginning estimate is always useful for comparison once a solution is found. The answer must be reasonable and must fulfill all requirements of the problem.

Presenting students with a variety of methods to solve the same type of math problem empowers each student to select the process that works best for them personally. It can help increase motivation and confidence to tackle difficult math problems. Just as there are different types of learners (visual, kinesthetic, etc.), so too are there particular problem-solving approaches that different students prefer or grasp more easily than others. Skilled mathematicians are versed in multiple methods to tackle various problems, with each method bolstering their toolbox with a strategy that can be employed for ease and efficiency when encountering math work.

Instead of focusing on the "right" way to solve a problem, teachers should strive to present multiple methods and explain the pros, cons, and appropriate applications for each method. For example, when trying to find the zeros in a binomial expression, one might be able to factor the expression, complete the square, use the quadratic equation, or make a rough sketch of the graph and identify the x-intercepts. In some cases, one method may not be possible and another may be "easiest," but by providing students with the various strategies, teachers enable them to be critical thinkers and select the method they deem most appropriate.

The following two examples demonstrate how different methods can be used for the same problem:

Example:

A store is having a spring sale, where everything is 70% off. You have $45.00 to spend. A jacket is regularly priced at $80.00. Do you have enough to buy the jacket and a pair of gloves, regularly priced at $20.00?

There are two ways to approach this.

Method 1:

Set up the equations to find the sale prices: the original price minus the amount discounted.
$80.00 - ($80.00 (0.70)) = sale cost of the jacket.
$20.00 – ($20.00 (0.70)) = sale cost of the gloves.
Solve for the sale cost.
$24.00 = sale cost of the jacket.
$6.00 = sale cost of the gloves.
Determine if you have enough money for both.
$24.00 + $6.00 = total sale cost.
$30.00 is less than $45.00, so you can afford to purchase both.

Method 2:

Determine the percent of the original price that you will pay.
100% – 70% = 30%
Set up the equations to find the sale prices.
$80.00 (0.30) = cost of the jacket.
$20.00 (0.30) = cost of the gloves.
Solve.
$24.00 = cost of the jacket.
$6.00 = cost of the gloves.
Determine if you have enough money for both.
$24.00 + $6.00 = total sale cost.
$30.00 is less than $45.00, so you can afford to purchase both.

Example:

Mary and Dottie team up to mow neighborhood lawns. If Mary mows 2 lawns per hour and the two of them can mow 17.5 lawns in 5 hours, how many lawns does Dottie mow per hour?

Given rate for Mary.

$$Mary = \frac{2\ lawns}{1\ hour}$$

Unknown rate of D for Dottie.

$$Dottie = \frac{D\ lawns}{1\ hour}$$

Given rate for both.

$$Total\ mowed\ together = \frac{17.5\ lawns}{5\ hours}$$

Set up the equation for what is being asked.

$$Mary + Dottie = total\ together.$$

Fill in the givens.

$$2 + D = \frac{17.5}{5}$$

Divide.

$$2 + D = 3.5$$

Subtract 2 from both sides to isolate the variable.

$$2 - 2 + D = 3.5 - 2$$

Solve and label Dottie's mowing rate.

$$D = 1.5\ lawns\ per\ hour$$

Numerical & Graphic Relationships

Relationships in Numerical Data

In some cases, it is useful to compare numerical data and determine the relationship between values. One of the best ways to mathematically compare two values is to compute the percentage difference between the two values. For example, consider a given music shop that had a net profit of $120,000 in the first year of operation and $185,000 over the second year. Rather than simply finding the net difference between the two years (using subtraction), the business owner may want to know by what percentage his profit increased; in other words, how much his profit in the second year increased relative to his first year. In such cases, the percentage change is desired. The following sections provide some guidance for this process.

Percent Increase/Decrease
Problems dealing with percentages may involve an original value, a change in that value, and a percentage change. A problem will provide two pieces of information and ask to find the third. To do so, this formula is used: $\frac{change}{original\ value}$ x 100 = percent change. Here's a sample problem:

> Attendance at a baseball stadium has dropped 16% from last year. Last year's average attendance was 40,000. What is this year's average attendance? (unknown).

Using the formula and information, the change is unknown (x), the original value is 40,000, and the percent change is 16%. The formula can be written as: $\frac{x}{40,000}$ x 100 = 16. When solving for x, it is determined the change was 6,400. The problem asked for this year's average attendance, so to calculate, the change (6,400) is subtracted from last year's attendance (40,000) to determine this year's average attendance is 33,600.

Percent More Than/Less Than
Percentage problems may give a value and what percent that given value is more than or less than an original unknown value. Here's a sample problem:

> A store advertises that all its merchandise has been reduced by 25%. The new price of a pair of shoes is $60. What was the original price?

This problem can be solved by writing a proportion. Two ratios should be written comparing the cost and the percent of the original cost. The new cost is 75% of the original cost (100% - 25%); and the original cost is 100% of the original cost. The unknown original cost can be represented by x. The proportion would be set up as: $\frac{60}{75} = \frac{x}{100}$. Solving the proportion, it is determined the original cost was $80.

The Position of Numbers Relative to Each Other

Place Value of a Digit
Numbers count in groups of 10. That number is the same throughout the set of natural numbers and whole numbers. It is referred to as working within a base 10 numeration system. Only the numbers from zero to 9 are used to represent any number. The foundation for doing this involves **place value**. Numbers are written side by side. This is to show the amount in each place value.

For place value, let's look at how the number 10 is different from zero to 9. It has two digits instead of just one. The one is in the tens' place, and the zero is in the ones' place. Therefore, there is one group of tens and zero ones. 11 has one 10 and one 1. The introduction of numbers from 11 to 19 should be the next step. Each value within this range of numbers consists of one group of 10 and a specific number of leftover ones. Counting by tens can be practiced once the tens column is understood. This process consists of increasing the number in the tens place by one. For example, counting by 10 starting at 17 would result in the next four values being 27, 37, 47, and 57.

A place value chart can be used for understanding and learning about numbers that have more digits. Here is an example of a place value chart:

	MILLIONS			THOUSANDS			ONES			.	DECIMALS		
billions	hundred millions	ten millions	millions	hundred thousands	ten thousands	thousands	hundreds	tens	ones	.	tenths	hundredths	thousandths

In the number 1,234, there are 4 ones and 3 tens. The 2 is in the hundreds' place, and the one is in the thousands' place. Note that each group of three digits is separated by a comma. The 2 has a value that is 10 times greater than the 3. Every place to the left has a value 10 times greater than the place to its right. Also, each group of three digits is also known as a *period*. 234 is in the ones' period.

The number 1,234 can be written out as *one-thousand, two hundred thirty-four*. The process of writing out numbers is known as the *decimal system*. It is also based on groups of 10. The place value chart is a helpful tool in using this system. In order to write out a number, it always starts with the digit(s) in the highest period. For example, in the number 23,815,467, the 23 is in highest place and is in the millions' period. The number is read *twenty-three million, eight hundred fifteen thousand, four hundred sixty-seven*. Each period is written separately through the use of commas. Also, no "ands" are used within the number. Another way to think about the number 23,815,467 is through the use of an addition problem. For example, $23,815,467 = 20,000,000 + 3,000,000 + 800,000 + 10,000 + 5,000 + 400 + 60 + 7$. This expression is known as *expanded form*. The actual number 23,815,467 is known as being in *standard form*.

In order to compare whole numbers with many digits, place value can be used. In each number to be compared, it is necessary to find the highest place value in which the numbers differ and to compare the value within that place value. For example, $4,523,345 < 4,532,456$ because of the values in the ten thousands place. A similar process can be used for decimals. However, number lines can also be used. Tick marks can be placed within two whole numbers on the number line that represent tenths, hundredths, etc. Each number being compared can then be plotted. The value farthest to the right on the number line is the largest.

Comparing, Classifying, and Ordering Real Numbers

Rational numbers are any number that can be written as a fraction or ratio. Within the set of rational numbers, several subsets exist that are referenced throughout the mathematics topics. **Counting numbers** are the first numbers learned as a child. Counting numbers consist of 1,2,3,4, and so on. **Whole numbers** include all counting numbers and zero (0,1,2,3,4,...). **Integers** include counting numbers, their opposites, and zero (...,-3,-2,-1,0,1,2,3,...). **Rational numbers** are inclusive of integers, fractions, and decimals that terminate, or end (1.7, 0.04213) or repeat (0.136$\bar{5}$).

A **number line** typically consists of integers (...3,2,1,0,-1,-2,-3...), and is used to visually represent the value of a rational number. Each rational number has a distinct position on the line determined by comparing its value with the displayed values on the line. For example, if plotting -1.5 on the number line below, it is necessary to recognize that the value of -1.5 is .5 less than -1 and .5 greater than -2. Therefore, -1.5 is plotted halfway between -1 and -2.

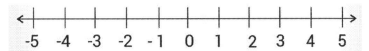

The number system that is used consists of only ten different digits or characters. However, this system is used to represent an infinite number of values. As mentioned, the **place value system** makes this infinite number of values possible. The position in which a digit is written corresponds to a given value. Starting from the decimal point (which is implied, if not physically present), each subsequent place value to the left represents a value greater than the one before it. Conversely, starting from the decimal point, each subsequent place value to the right represents a value less than the one before it.

In accordance with the **base-10 system**, the value of a digit increases by a factor of ten each place it moves to the left. For example, consider the number 7. Moving the digit one place to the left (70), increases its value by a factor of 10 ($7 \times 10 = 70$). Moving the digit two places to the left (700) increases its value by a factor of 10 twice ($7 \times 10 \times 10 = 700$). Moving the digit three places to the left (7,000) increases its value by a factor of 10 three times ($7 \times 10 \times 10 \times 10 = 7,000$), and so on.

Conversely, the value of a digit decreases by a factor of ten each place it moves to the right. (Note that multiplying by $\frac{1}{10}$ is equivalent to dividing by 10). For example, consider the number 40. Moving the digit one place to the right (4) decreases its value by a factor of 10 ($40 \div 10 = 4$). Moving the digit two places to the right (0.4), decreases its value by a factor of 10 twice ($40 \div 10 \div 10 = 0.4$) or ($40 \times \frac{1}{10} \times \frac{1}{10} = 0.4$). Moving the digit three places to the right (0.04) decreases its value by a factor of 10 three times ($40 \div 10 \div 10 \div 10 = 0.04$) or ($40 \times \frac{1}{10} \times \frac{1}{10} \times \frac{1}{10} = 0.04$), and so on.

Ordering Numbers

A common question type asks to order rational numbers from least to greatest or greatest to least. The numbers will come in a variety of formats, including decimals, percentages, roots, fractions, and whole numbers. These questions test for knowledge of different types of numbers and the ability to determine their respective values.

Before discussing ordering all numbers, let's start with decimals.

To compare decimals and order them by their value, utilize a method similar to that of ordering large numbers.

The main difference is where the comparison will start. Assuming that any numbers to left of the decimal point are equal, the next numbers to be compared are those immediately to the right of the decimal point. If those are equal, then move on to compare the values in the next decimal place to the right.

For example:

Which number is greater, 12.35 or 12.38?

Check that the values to the left of the decimal point are equal:

$$12 = 12$$

Next, compare the values of the decimal place to the right of the decimal:

$$12.3 = 12.3$$

Those are also equal in value.

Finally, compare the value of the numbers in the next decimal place to the right on both numbers:

$$12.3\mathbf{5} \text{ and } 12.3\mathbf{8}$$

Here the 5 is less than the 8, so the final way to express this inequality is:

$$12.35 < 12.38$$

Comparing decimals is regularly exemplified with money because the "cents" portion of money ends in the hundredths place. When paying for gasoline or meals in restaurants, and even in bank accounts, if enough errors are made when calculating numbers to the hundredths place, they can add up to dollars and larger amounts of money over time.

Now that decimal ordering has been explained, let's expand and consider all real numbers. Whether the question asks to order the numbers from greatest to least or least to greatest, the crux of the question is the same—convert the numbers into a common format. Generally, it's easiest to write the numbers as whole numbers and decimals so they can be placed on a number line. Follow these examples to understand this strategy.

1) Order the following rational numbers from greatest to least:

$$\sqrt{36}, 0.65, 78\%, \frac{3}{4}, 7, 90\%, \frac{5}{2}$$

Of the seven numbers, the whole number (7) and decimal (0.65) are already in an accessible form, so concentrate on the other five.

First, the square root of 36 equals 6. (If the test asks for the root of a non-perfect root, determine which two whole numbers the root lies between.) Next, convert the percentages to decimals. A percentage means "per hundred," so this conversion requires moving the decimal point two places to the left, leaving 0.78 and 0.9.

Lastly, evaluate the fractions:

$$\frac{3}{4} = \frac{75}{100} = 0.75 \; ; \frac{5}{2} = 2\frac{1}{2} = 2.5$$

Now, the only step left is to list the numbers in the request order:

$$7, \sqrt{36}, \frac{5}{2}, 90\%, 78\%, \frac{3}{4}, 0.65$$

2) Order the following rational numbers from least to greatest:

$$2.5, \sqrt{9}, \text{-}10.5, 0.853, 175\%, \sqrt{4}, \frac{4}{5}$$

$$\sqrt{9} = 3$$

$$175\% = 1.75$$

$$\sqrt{4} = 2$$

$$\frac{4}{5} = 0.8$$

From least to greatest, the answer is:

$$\text{-}10.5, \frac{4}{5}, 0.853, 175\%, \sqrt{4}, 2.5, \sqrt{9}$$

Expressing Numeric Relationships

If a question asks to give words to a mathematical expression and says "equals," then an = sign must be included in the answer. Similarly, "less than or equal to" is expressed by the inequality symbol ≤, and "greater than or equal" to is expressed as ≥. Furthermore, "less than" is represented by <, and "greater than" is expressed by >.

Equations use the equals sign because the numeric expressions on either side of the symbol (=) are equivalent. In contrast, inequalities compare values or expressions that are unequal. Although not always true, linear equations that include a variable often have just one value for the variable that makes the statement true. Linear inequalities generally have an infinite number of values that make the statement true.

Inequalities are a concise mathematical way to express the relationship between unequal values. More specifically, they describe in what way the values are unequal. A value could be greater than (>); less than (<); greater than or equal to (≥); or less than or equal to (≤) another value. The statement "five times a number added to forty is more than sixty-five" can be expressed as $5x + 40 > 65$. Common words and phrases that express inequalities are:

Symbol	Phrase
<	is under, is below, smaller than, beneath
>	is above, is over, bigger than, exceeds
≤	no more than, at most, maximum
≥	no less than, at least, minimum

Solving Linear Inequalities

When solving a linear inequality, the solution is the set of all numbers that makes the statement true. The inequality $x + 2 \geq 6$ has a solution set of 4 and every number greater than 4 (4.0001, 5, 12, 107, etc.). Adding 2 to 4 or any number greater than 4 would result in a value that is greater than or equal to 6. Therefore, $x \geq 4$ would be the solution set.

Solution sets for linear inequalities often will be displayed using a number line. If a value is included in the set ($\geq$ or $\leq$), there is a shaded dot placed on that value and an arrow extending in the direction of the solutions. For a variable $>$ or $\geq$ a number, the arrow would point right on the number line (the direction where the numbers increase); and if a variable is $<$ or $\leq$ a number, the arrow would point left (where the numbers decrease). If the value is not included in the set ($>$ or $<$), an open circle on that value would be used with an arrow in the appropriate direction.

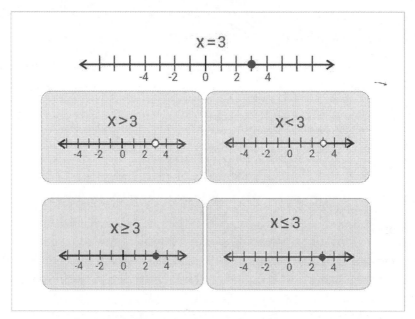

Students may be asked to write a linear inequality given a graph of its solution set. To do so, they should identify whether the value is included (shaded dot or open circle) and the direction in which the arrow is pointing.

In order to algebraically solve a linear inequality, the same steps should be followed as in solving a linear equation. The inequality symbol stays the same for all operations EXCEPT when dividing by a negative number. If dividing by a negative number while solving an inequality, the relationship reverses (the sign flips). Dividing by a positive does not change the relationship, so the sign stays the same. In other words, $>$ switches to $<$ and vice versa. An example is shown below.

Solve $-2(x + 4) \leq 22$

Distribute: $-2x - 8 \leq 22$

Add 8 to both sides: $-2x \leq 30$

Divide both sides by -2: $x \geq 15$

Mathematically Equivalent Expressions

It is helpful to be skilled at identifying values that are equivalent but that are expressed in different forms, such as a fraction, decimal, and percent, because it enables one to convert the representation of a value for easier calculation in a given problem. Manipulating values is often required when working with percentages in order to carry out calculations. The word percent means "per hundred." When dealing with percentages, it may be helpful to think of the number as a value in hundredths. For example, 15% can be expressed as "fifteen hundredths" and written as $\frac{15}{100}$ or .15.

Converting from Decimals and Fractions to Percentages
To convert a decimal to a percent, a number is multiplied by 100. To write .25 as a percent, the equation .25 × 100 yields 25%. To convert a fraction to a percent, the fraction is converted to a decimal and then multiplied by 100. To convert $\frac{3}{5}$ to a decimal, the numerator (3) is divided by the denominator (5). This results in .6, which is then multiplied by 100 to get 60%.

To convert a percent to a decimal, the number is divided by 100. For example, 150% is equal to 1.5 $\left(\frac{150}{100}\right)$. To convert a percent to a fraction, the percent sign is deleted and the value is written as the numerator with a denominator of 100. For example, 2% = $\frac{2}{100}$. Fractions should be reduced: $\frac{2}{100} = \frac{1}{50}$.

Rounding Rules

As mentioned, rounding is an important concept dealing with place value. **Rounding** is the process of either bumping a number up or down, based on a certain place value.

Rounding numbers consists of:

- determining what place value the number is being rounded to
- examining the digit to the right of the desired place value to decide whether to round up or keep the digit, and
- replacing all digits to the right of the desired place value with zeros.

To round 746,311 to the nearest ten thousand, the digit in the ten thousands place should be located first. In this case, this digit is 4 (7<u>4</u>6,311). Then, the digit to its right is examined. If this digit is 5 or greater, the number will be rounded up by increasing the digit in the desired place by one. If the digit to the right of the place value being rounded is 4 or less, the number will be kept the same. For the given example, the digit being examined is a 6, which means that the number will be rounded up by increasing the digit to the left by one. Therefore, the digit 4 is changed to a 5. Finally, to write the rounded number, any digits to the left of the place value being rounded remain the same and any to its right are replaced with zeros. For the given example, rounding 746,311 to the nearest ten thousand will produce 750,000. To round 746,311 to the nearest hundred, the digit to the right of the three in the hundreds place is examined to determine whether to round up or keep the same number. In this case, that digit is a 1, so the number will be kept the same and any digits to its right will be replaced with zeros. The resulting rounded number is 746,300.

Rounding place values to the right of the decimal follows the same procedure, but digits being replaced by zeros can simply be dropped. To round 3.752891 to the nearest thousandth, the desired place value is located (3.75<u>2</u>891) and the digit to the right is examined. In this case, the digit 8 indicates that the number will be rounded up, and the 2 in the thousandths place will increase to a 3. Rounding up and replacing the digits to the right of the thousandths place produces 3.753000 which is equivalent to 3.753. Therefore, the zeros are not necessary and the rounded number should be written as 3.753.

When rounding up, if the digit to be increased is a 9, the digit to its left is increased by 1 and the digit in the desired place value is changed to a zero. For example, the number 1,598 rounded to the nearest ten is 1,600. Another example shows the number 43.72961 rounded to the nearest thousandth is 43.730 or 43.73.

Logical Connectives and Quantifiers

Logical connectives such as *and, or if,* and *then,* are often used with deductive reasoning. This type of reasoning in math involves starting with stating a general rule, and then moving forward with logic to obtain a desired conclusion. If the original statements are true, then the conclusion is true. Most of mathematics involves deductive reasoning. For example, if $x = 2$ and $y = 4$ then $x + y = 6$. Also, if x is an even number and y is an odd number, then $x + y$ is an odd number.

Quantifiers may also be encountered in mathematical problems. The quantifier *all* means that the rule applies across the board or universally or that the entire number of something is present or true. For example, *all* pentagons have five angles. In contrast, the quantifier *none* indicates that not a single one of the items or values in the statement make the statement true or fit the criteria. For example, *none* of the angles in an equilateral triangle are obtuse. The vague quantifier *some* treads the middle ground between those two extremes, and means that an unspecified number or amount of something applies or makes the statement true. For example, the whole amount or number of." For example, *some* rectangles are squares.

Filling in Missing Values in a Data Table

Missing values in a table can be calculated by determining if there is a formula to represent the relationship among values or levels in the table or if empty cells denote subtotals. For example, if a data table presents an itemized list of the type and number of items purchased and the unit price of each item, the subtotal for the cost of each type of item can be calculated by multiplying the number of that item purchased by the unit price.

Consider the table presented earlier of Walter's expenses. This time, several of the "total cost" cells are blank:

Item	Quantity	Cost Per Unit	Total Cost
Hot Coffee	200	$0.25	$50
Slow-Drip Iced Coffee	100	$0.75	
Latte	50		$50
Muffin	75	$1.00	$75
Crepe		$2.00	$90
Egg Sandwich	60	$3.00	$180
Utilities, rent, and labor			$500
Total Costs			$1,020

The total cost for slow-drip iced coffee can be calculated by multiplying the quantity (100) by the cost per unit ($0.75): $100 \times \$0.75 = \$75$. The cost per unit for a latte can be calculated by dividing the total cost ($50) by the number of lattes sold (50): $50 ÷ 50 = 1.00. The number of crepes sold can be found in the same manner, but this time, the total cost is divided by the unit cost: $90 ÷ $2.00 = 45 \ crepes$.

Using Information from Tables and Graphs to Solve Problems

Data can be represented in many ways. It is important to be able to organize the data into categories that could be represented using one of these methods. Equally important is the ability to read these types of diagrams and interpret their meaning.

Data in Tables

One of the most common ways to express data is in a table. The primary reason for plugging data into a table is to make interpretation more convenient. It's much easier to look at the table than to analyze results in a narrative paragraph. When analyzing a table, pay close attention to the title, variables, and data.

Let's analyze a theoretical antibiotic study. The study has 6 groups, named A through F, and each group receives a different dose of medicine. The results of the study are listed in the table below.

Results of Antibiotic Studies		
Group	Dosage of Antibiotics in milligrams (mg)	Efficacy (% of participants cured)
A	0 mg	20%
B	20 mg	40%
C	40 mg	75%
D	60 mg	95%
E	80 mg	100%
F	100 mg	100%

Tables generally list the title immediately above the data. The title should succinctly explain what is listed below. Here, "Results of Antibiotic Studies" informs the audience that the data pertains to the results of scientific study on antibiotics.

Identifying the variables at play is one of the most important parts of interpreting data. Remember, the independent variable is intentionally altered, and its change is independent of the other variables. Here, the dosage of antibiotics administered to the different groups is the independent variable. The study is intentionally manipulating the strength of the medicine to study the related results. Efficacy is the dependent variable since its results *depend* on a different variable, the dose of antibiotics. Generally, the independent variable will be listed before the dependent variable in tables.

Also play close attention to the variables' labels. Here, the dose is expressed in milligrams (mg) and efficacy in percentages (%). Keep an eye out for questions referencing data in a different unit measurement, as discussed in the next topic, or questions asking for a raw number when only the percentage is listed.

Now that the nature of the study and variables at play have been identified, the data itself needs be interpreted. Group A did not receive any of the medicine. As discussed earlier, Group A is the control, as it reflects the amount of people cured in the same timeframe without medicine. It's important to see that efficacy positively correlates with the dosage of medicine. A question using this study might ask for the lowest dose of antibiotics to achieve 100% efficacy. Although Group E and Group F both achieve 100% efficacy, it's important to note that Group E reaches 100% with a lower dose.

Data is often recorded using fractions, such as half a mile, and understanding fractions is critical because of their popular use in real-world applications. Also, it is extremely important to label values with their units when using data. For example, regarding length, the number 2 is meaningless unless it is attached to a unit. Writing 2 cm shows that the number refers to the length of an object.

<u>Data in Graphs</u>
Graphs provide a visual representation of data. The variables are placed on the two axes. The bottom of the graph is referred to as the horizontal axis or X-axis. The left-hand side of the graph is known as the vertical axis or Y-axis. Typically, the independent variable is placed on the X-axis, and the dependent variable is located on the Y-axis. Sometimes the X-axis is a timeline, and the dependent variables for different trials or groups have been measured throughout points in time; time is still an independent variable, but is not always immediately thought of as the independent variable being studied.

The most common types of graphs are the bar graph and the line graph.

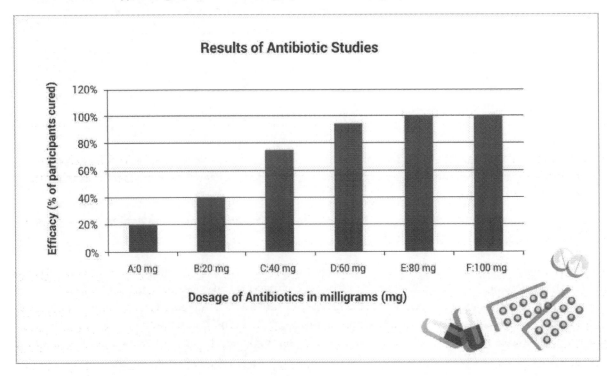

The **bar graph** above expresses the data from the table entitled "Results of Antibiotic Studies." To interpret the data for each group in the study, look at the top of their bars and read the corresponding efficacy on the Y-axis.

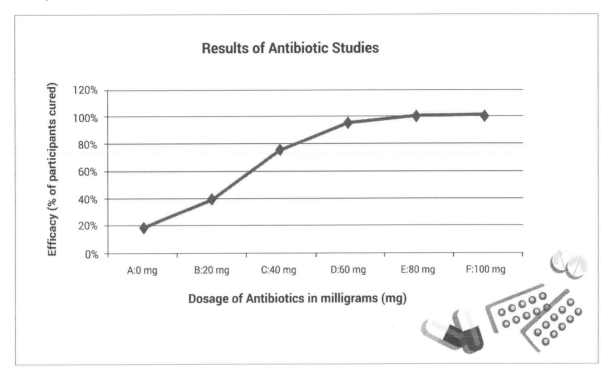

Here, the same data is expressed on a **line graph**. The points on the line correspond with each data entry. Reading the data on the line graph works like the bar graph. The data trend is measured by the slope of the line.

Data in Other Charts
Chart is a broad term that refers to a variety of ways to represent data.

To graph relations, the **Cartesian plane** is used. This means to think of the plane as being given a grid of squares, with one direction being the x-axis and the other direction the y-axis. Generally, the independent variable is placed along the horizontal axis, and the dependent variable is placed along the vertical axis. Any point on the plane can be specified by saying how far to go along the x-axis and how far along the y-axis with a pair of numbers (x, y). Specific values for these pairs can be given names such as $C = (-1, 3)$. Negative values mean to move left or down; positive values mean to move right or up. The point where the axes cross one another is called the **origin**. The origin has coordinates $(0, 0)$ and is usually called O when given a specific label.

An illustration of the Cartesian plane, along with graphs of $(2, 1)$ and $(-1, -1)$, are below.

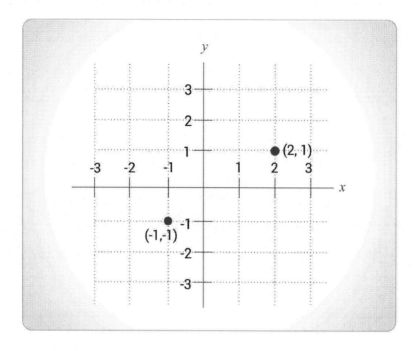

A **box plot**, also called a **box-and-whisker plot**, divides the data points into four groups and displays the five number summary for the set, as well as any outliers. The five number summary consists of:

- The lower extreme: the lowest value that is not an outlier
- The higher extreme: the highest value that is not an outlier
- The median of the set: also referred to as the second quartile or Q_2
- The first quartile or Q_1: the median of values below Q_2
- The third quartile or Q_3: the median of values above Q_2

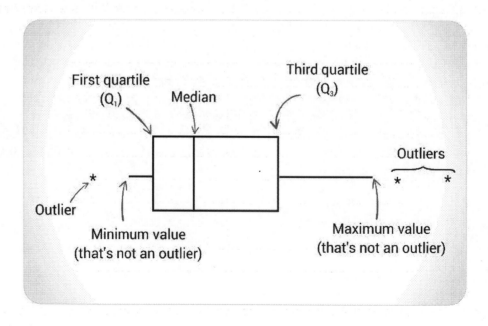

Suppose the box plot displays IQ scores for 12th grade students at a given school. The five number summary of the data consists of: lower extreme (67); upper extreme (127); Q_2 or median (100); Q_1 (91); Q_3 (108); and outliers (135 and 140). Although all data points are not known from the plot, the points are divided into four quartiles each, including 25% of the data points. Therefore, 25% of students scored between 67 and 91, 25% scored between 91 and 100, 25% scored between 100 and 108, and 25% scored between 108 and 127. These percentages include the normal values for the set and exclude the outliers. This information is useful when comparing a given score with the rest of the scores in the set.

A **line plot** is a diagram that shows quantity of data along a number line. It is a quick way to record data in a structure similar to a bar graph without needing to do the required shading of a bar graph. Here is an example of a line plot:

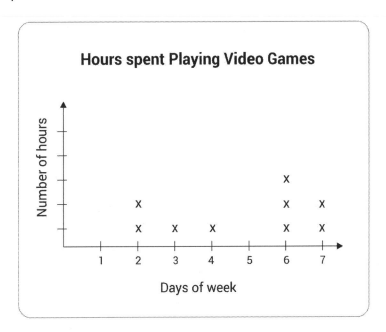

A **tally chart** is a diagram in which tally marks are utilized to represent data. Tally marks are a means of showing a quantity of objects within a specific classification. Here is an example of a tally chart:

Number of days with rain	Number of weeks
0	II
1	⊪Ħ
2	⊪Ħ
3	ĦĦ
4	ĦĦ ĦĦ ĦĦ IIII
5	ĦĦ I
6	ĦĦ I
7	IIII

A **picture graph** is a diagram that shows pictorial representation of data being discussed. The symbols used can represent a certain number of objects. Notice how each fruit symbol in the following graph represents a count of two fruits. One drawback of picture graphs is that they can be less accurate if each symbol represents a large number. For example, if each banana symbol represented ten bananas, and students consumed 22 bananas, it may be challenging to draw and interpret two and one-fifth bananas as a frequency count of 22.

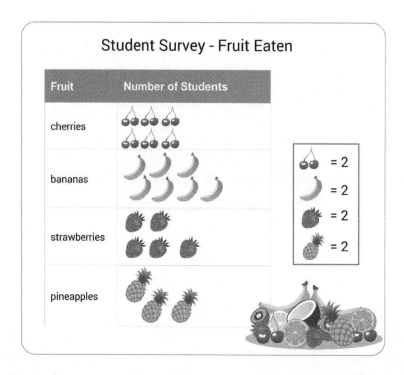

A **circle graph**, also called a **pie chart**, shows categorical data with each category representing a percentage of the whole data set. To make a circle graph, the percent of the data set for each category must be determined. To do so, the frequency of the category is divided by the total number of data points and converted to a percent. For example, if 80 people were asked what their favorite sport is and 20 responded basketball, basketball makes up 25% of the data ($\frac{20}{80} = .25 = 25\%$). Each category in a data set is represented by a *slice* of the circle proportionate to its percentage of the whole.

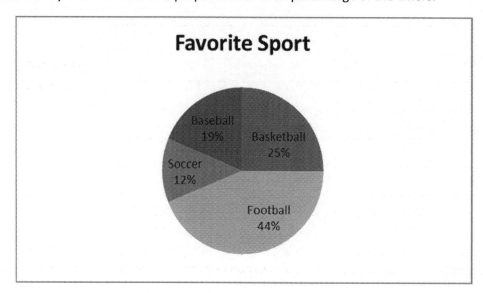

A **scatterplot** displays the relationship between two variables. Values for the independent variable, typically denoted by x, are paired with values for the dependent variable, typically denoted by y. Each set of corresponding values are written as an ordered pair (x, y). To construct the graph, a coordinate grid is labeled with the x-axis representing the independent variable and the y-axis representing the dependent variable. Each ordered pair is graphed.

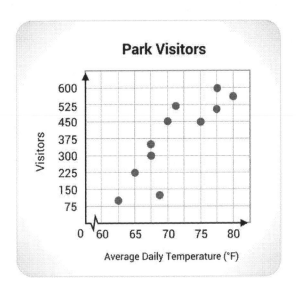

Like a scatter plot, a **line graph** compares two variables that change continuously, typically over time. Paired data values (ordered pair) are plotted on a coordinate grid with the x- and y-axis representing the two variables. A line is drawn from each point to the next, going from left to right. A double line graph simply displays two sets of data that contain values for the same two variables. The double line graph below displays the profit for given years (two variables) for Company A and Company B (two data sets).

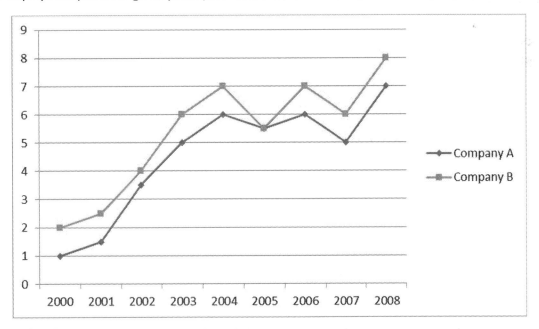

Scatter plots and line graphs can be used to display data consisting of two variables. Examples include height and weight, or distance and time. A correlation between the variables is determined by examining the points on the graph. Line graphs are used if each value for one variable pairs with a distinct value for the other variable. Line graphs show relationships between variables.

Choosing the appropriate graph to display a data set depends on what type of data is included in the set and what information must be shown. Histograms and box plots can be used for data sets consisting of individual values across a wide range. Examples include test scores and incomes. Histograms and box plots will indicate the center, spread, range, and outliers of a data set. A histogram will show the shape of the data set, while a box plot will divide the set into quartiles (25% increments), allowing for comparison between a given value and the entire set.

Scatter plots and line graphs can be used to display data consisting of two variables. Examples include height and weight, or distance and time. A correlation between the variables is determined by examining the points on the graph. Line graphs are used if each value for one variable pairs with a distinct value for the other variable. Line graphs show relationships between variables.

Drawing Conclusions Based on Graphical Displays

Comparing data sets within statistics can mean many things. The first way to compare data sets is by looking at the center and spread of each set. The **center of a data** set can mean two things: median or mean. The **median** is the value that's halfway into each data set, and it splits the data into two intervals. The **mean** is the average value of the data within a set. It's calculated by adding up all of the data in the set and dividing the total by the number of data points. Outliers can significantly impact the mean. Additionally, two completely different data sets can have the same mean. For example, a data set with values ranging from 0 to 100 and a data set with values ranging from 44 to 56 can both have means of 50. The first data set has a much wider range, which is known as the **spread** of the data. This measures how varied the data is within each set.

In an experiment, variables are the key to analyzing data, especially when data is in a graph or table. Variables can represent anything, including objects, conditions, events, and amounts of time.

Covariance is a general term referring to how two variables move in relation to each other. Take for example an employee that gets paid by the hour. For them, hours worked and total pay have a positive covariance. As hours worked increases, so does pay.

Constant variables remain unchanged by the scientist across all trials. Because they are held constant for all groups in an experiment, they aren't being measured in the experiment, and they are usually ignored. Constants can either be controlled by the scientist directly like the nutrition, water, and sunlight given to plants, or they can be selected by the scientist specifically for an experiment like using a certain animal species or choosing to investigate only people of a certain age group.

Independent variables are also controlled by the scientist, but they are the same only for each group or trial in the experiment. Each group might be composed of students that all have the same color of car or each trial may be run on different soda brands. The independent variable of an experiment is what is being indirectly tested because it causes change in the dependent variables.

Dependent variables experience change caused by the independent variable and are what is being measured or observed. For example, college acceptance rates could be a dependent variable of an experiment that sorted a large sample of high school students by an independent variable such as test scores. In this experiment, the scientist groups the high school students by the independent variable (test scores) to see how it affects the dependent variable (their college acceptance rates).

Note that most variables can be held constant in one experiment but independent or dependent in another. For example, when testing how well a fertilizer aids plant growth, its amount of sunlight should be held constant for each group of plants, but if the experiment is being done to determine the proper amount of sunlight a plant should have, the amount of sunlight is an independent variable because it is necessarily changed for each group of plants.

An **X-Y diagram**, also known as a **scatter diagram**, visually displays the relationship between two variables. The independent variable is placed on the *x-axis*, or horizontal axis, and the dependent variable is placed on the *y-axis*, or vertical axis.

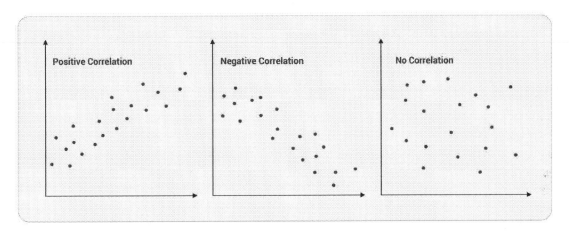

As shown in the figures above, an X-Y diagram may result in positive, negative, or no correlation between the two variables. So in the first scatter plot as the Y factor increases the X factor increases as well. The opposite is true as well: as the X factor increases the Y factor also increases. Thus there is a positive correlation because one factor appears to positively affect the other factor

It's important to note, however, that finding a significant relationship between the dependent variable and the independent variable does not necessarily imply that there is a causal relationship between the two variables. It only means that once the independent variable is known, a fairly accurate prediction of the dependent variable can be made. This is often expressed with the phrase *correlation does not imply causation*. In other words, just because there is a relationship between two variables does not mean that one is the cause of the other. There could be other factors involved that are the real cause. For example, a positive correlation between labor hours and units produced may not equate to a cause and effect relationship between the two. Any instance of correlation only indicates how likely the presence of one variable is in the instance of another. The variables should be further analyzed to determine which, if any, other variables (i.e. quality of employee work) may contribute to the positive correlation.

As another example of the phenomenon that correlation does not imply causation, consider an experiment where the independent variable is the value of a person's house, and the dependent variable is their income. Although people in more expensive houses are expected to make more money, it is clear that their expensive houses are not the cause of them making more money. This illustrates one example of why it is important for experimenters to be careful when drawing conclusions about causation from their data.

Linear Data Fitting
The simplest type of correlation between two variables is a **linear correlation**. If the independent variable is x and the dependent variable is y, then a linear correlation means $y = mx + b$. If m is

positive, then y will increase as x increases. While if m is negative, then y decreases while x increases. The variable b represents the value of y when x is 0.

As one example of such a correlation, consider a manufacturing plant. Suppose x is the number of units produced by the plant, and y is the cost to the company. In this example, b will be the cost of the plant itself. The plant will cost money even if it is never used, just by buying the machinery. For each unit produced, there will be a cost for the labor and the material. Let m represent this cost to produce one unit of the product.

For a more concrete example, suppose a computer factory costs \$100,000. It requires \$100 of parts and \$50 of labor to make one computer. How much will it cost for a company to make 1000 computers? To figure this, let y be the amount of money the company spends, and let x be the number of computers. The cost of the factory is \$100,000, so $b = 100,000$. On the other hand, the cost of producing a computer is the parts plus labor, or \$150, so $m = 150$. Therefore, $y = 150x + 100,000$. Substitute 1000 for x and get $y = 150 \times 1000 + 100,000 = 150,000 + 1000 = 250,000$. It will cost the company \$250,000 to make 1000 computers.

Interpreting Competing Data
Be careful of questions with competing studies. These questions will ask to interpret which of two studies shows the greater amount or the higher rate of change between two results.

Here's an example. A research facility runs studies on two different antibiotics: Drug A and Drug B. The Drug A study includes 1,000 participants and cures 600 people. The Drug B study includes 200 participants and cures 150 people. Which drug is more successful?

The first step is to determine the percentage of each drug's rate of success. Drug A was successful in curing 60% of participants, while Drug B achieved a 75% success rate. Thus, Drug B is more successful based on these studies, even though it cured fewer people.

Sample size and experiment consistency should also be considered when answering questions based on competing studies. Is one study significantly larger than the other? In the antibiotics example, the Drug A study is five times larger than Drug B. Thus, Drug B's higher efficacy (desired result) could be a result of the smaller sample size, rather than the quality of drug.

Consistency between studies is directly related to sample size. Let's say the research facility elects to conduct more studies on Drug B. In the next study, there are 400 participants, and 200 are cured. The success rate of the second study is 50%. The results are clearly inconsistent with the first study, which means more testing is needed to determine the drug's efficacy. A hallmark of mathematical or scientific research is repeatability. Studies should be consistent and repeatable, with an appropriately large sample size, before drawing extensive conclusions.

CBEST Math Practice Test #1

1. Which of the following numbers has the greatest value?
   a. 1.4378
   b. 1.07548
   c. 1.43592
   d. 0.89409
   e. 1.43688

2. The value of 6 x 12 is the same as which of the following?
   a. 2 x 4 x 4 x 2
   b. 7 x 4 x 3
   c. 6 x 6 x 3
   d. 3 x 3 x 4 x 2
   e. 3 x 4 x 6 x 2

3. This chart indicates how many sales of CDs, vinyl records, and MP3 downloads occurred over the last year. Approximately what percentage of the total sales was from CDs?

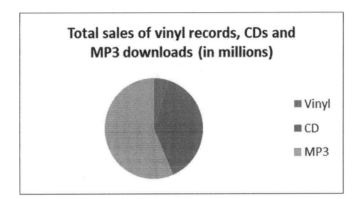

   a. 55%
   b. 25%
   c. 40%
   d. 5%
   e. 20%

4. After a 20% sale discount, Frank purchased a new refrigerator for $850. How much did he save from the original price?
   a. $170
   b. $212.50
   c. $105.75
   d. $200
   e. $150

5. A student gets an 85% on a test with 20 questions. How many answers did the student solve correctly?
    a. 16
    b. 15
    c. 18
    d. 19
    e. 17

6. Simplify the following fraction:

$$\frac{\frac{5}{7}}{\frac{9}{11}}$$

    a. $\frac{55}{63}$

    b. $\frac{7}{1000}$

    c. $\frac{13}{15}$

    d. $\frac{5}{11}$

    e. $\frac{11}{9}$

7. Johnny earns $2334.50 from his job each month. He pays $1437 for monthly expenses. Johnny is planning a vacation in 3 months' time that he estimates will cost $1750 total. How much will Johnny have left over from three months' of saving once he pays for his vacation?
    a. $948.50
    b. $584.50
    c. $852.50
    d. $942.50
    e. $952.50

8. What is $\frac{420}{98}$ rounded to the nearest integer?
    a. 3
    b. 4
    c. 5
    d. 6
    e. 7

9. Dwayne has received the following scores on his math tests: 78, 92, 83, 97. What score must Dwayne get on his next math test to have an overall average of at least 90?
    a. 89
    b. 98
    c. 95
    d. 100
    e. 96

10. What is the overall median of Dwayne's current scores: 78, 92, 83, 97?
   a. 19
   b. 85
   c. 83
   d. 87.5
   e. 86

11. Solve the following:

$$(\sqrt{36} \times \sqrt{16}) - 3^2$$

Radical

   a. 30
   b. 21
   c. 15
   d. 13
   e. 16

12. In Jim's school, there are 3 girls for every 2 boys. There are 650 students in total. Using this information, how many students are girls?
   a. 260
   b. 130
   c. 65
   d. 390
   e. 225

13. Five of six numbers have a sum of 25. The average of all six numbers is 6. What is the sixth number?
   a. 8
   b. 12
   c. 13
   d. 10
   e. 11

14. Kimberley earns $10 an hour babysitting, and after 10 p.m., she earns $12 an hour, with the amount paid being rounded to the nearest hour accordingly. On her last job, she worked from 5:30 p.m. to 11 p.m. In total, how much did Kimberley earn on her last job?
   a. $45
   b. $57
   c. $62
   d. $42
   e. $67

15. Arrange the following numbers from least to greatest value:

$0.85, \frac{4}{5}, \frac{2}{3}, \frac{91}{100}$

    a. $0.85, \frac{4}{5}, \frac{2}{3}, \frac{91}{100}$

    b. $\frac{4}{5}, 0.85, \frac{91}{100}, \frac{2}{3}$

    c. $\frac{2}{3}, \frac{4}{5}, 0.85, \frac{91}{100}$

    d. $0.85, \frac{91}{100}, \frac{4}{5}, \frac{2}{3}$

    e. $\frac{4}{5}, \frac{2}{3}, 0.85, \frac{91}{100}$

16. A ball is drawn at random from a ball pit containing 8 red balls, 7 yellow balls, 6 green balls, and 5 purple balls. What's the probability that the ball drawn is yellow?
    a. $^1/_{26}$
    b. $^{19}/_{26}$
    c. $^{14}/_{26}$
    d. 1
    e. $^7/_{26}$

17. Two cards are drawn from a shuffled deck of 52 cards. What's the probability that both cards are Kings if the first card isn't replaced after it's drawn and is a King?
    a. $^1/_{169}$
    b. $^1/_{221}$
    c. $^1/_{13}$
    d. $^4/_{13}$
    e. $^1/_{104}$

18. Four people split a bill. The first person pays for $\frac{1}{5}$, the second person pays for $\frac{1}{4}$, and the third person pays for $\frac{1}{3}$. What fraction of the bill does the fourth person pay?
    a. $\frac{13}{60}$

    b. $\frac{47}{60}$

    c. $\frac{1}{4}$

    d. $\frac{4}{15}$

    e. $\frac{1}{2}$

19. Simplify the following expression:

$$4\frac{2}{3} - 3\frac{4}{9}$$

    a. $1\frac{1}{3}$

    b. $1\frac{2}{9}$

    c. 1

    d. $1\frac{2}{3}$

    e. $1\frac{4}{9}$

20. A closet is filled with red, blue, and green shirts. If $\frac{1}{3}$ of the shirts are green and $\frac{2}{5}$ are red, what fraction of the shirts are blue?

    a. $\frac{4}{15}$

    b. $\frac{1}{5}$

    c. $\frac{7}{15}$

    d. $\frac{1}{2}$

    e. $\frac{2}{3}$

21. Shawna buys $2\frac{1}{2}$ gallons of paint. If she uses $\frac{1}{3}$ of it on the first day, how much does she have left?

    a. $1\frac{5}{6}$ gallons

    b. $1\frac{1}{2}$ gallons

    c. $1\frac{2}{3}$ gallons

    d. 2 gallons

    e. $1\frac{3}{4}$ gallons

22. Jessica buys 10 cans of paint. Red paint costs \$1 per can and blue paint costs \$2 per can. In total, she spends \$16. How many red cans did she buy?

    a. 2

    b. 3

    c. 4

    d. 5

    e. 6

23. Six people apply to work for Janice's company, but she only needs four workers. How many different groups of four employees can Janice choose?

    a. 6

    b. 10

    c. 15

    d. 36

    e. 30

24. Which of the following is equivalent to the value of the digit 3 in the number 792.134?

    a. 3×10

    b. 3×100

    c. $\dfrac{3}{10}$

    d. $\dfrac{3}{100}$

    e. 3×0.1

25. In the following expression, which operation should be completed first? $5 \times 6 + (5 + 4) \div 2 - 1$.

    a. Multiplication

    b. Addition

    c. Division

    d. Subtraction

    e. Parentheses

26. How will the number 847.89632 be written if rounded to the nearest hundredth?

    a. 847.90

    b. 900

    c. 847.89

    d. 847.896

    e. 847.895

27. The perimeter of a 6-sided polygon is 56 cm. The length of three of the sides are 9 cm each. The length of two other sides are 8 cm each. What is the length of the missing side?

    a. 11 cm

    b. 12 cm

    c. 13 cm

    d. 10 cm

    e. 9 cm

28. Which of the following is a mixed number?

   a. $16\frac{1}{2}$

   b. 16

   c. $\frac{16}{3}$

   d. $\frac{1}{4}$

   e. $\frac{3}{6}$

29. If you were showing your friend how to round 245.2678 to the nearest thousandth, which place value would be used to decide whether to round up or round down?
   a. Ten-thousandth
   b. Thousandth
   c. Hundredth
   d. Thousands
   e. Ones

30. What is the value of *b* in this equation?

$5b - 4 = 2b + 17$

   a. 13
   b. 24
   c. 7
   d. 21
   e. 14

31. Express the solution to the following problem in decimal form:

$$\frac{3}{5} \times \frac{7}{10} \div \frac{1}{2}$$

   a. 0.042
   b. 84%
   c. 0.84
   d. 0.42
   e. .084

32. What is an equivalent measurement for 1.3 cm?
   a. 0.13 m
   b. 0.013 m
   c. 0.13 mm
   d. 0.013 mm
   e. 1.13 mm

33. Katie works at a clothing company and sold 192 shirts over the weekend. $\frac{1}{3}$ of the shirts that were sold were patterned, and the rest were solid. Which mathematical expression would calculate the number of solid shirts Katie sold over the weekend?

    a. $192 \times \frac{1}{3}$

    b. $192 \div \frac{1}{3}$

    c. $192 \times (1 - \frac{1}{3})$

    d. $192 \div 3$

    e. $192 \div \left(1 - \frac{1}{3}\right)$

34. Which four-sided shape is always a rectangle?

    a. Rhombus

    b. Square

    c. Parallelogram

    d. Quadrilateral

    e. Trapezoid

35. A rectangle was formed out of pipe cleaner. Its length was $\frac{1}{2}$ ft, and its width was $\frac{11}{2}$ inches. What is its area in square inches?

    a. $\frac{11}{4}$ inch^2

    b. $\frac{11}{2}$ inch^2

    c. 22 inches^2

    d. 33 inches^2

    e. 11 inches^2

36. How will $\frac{4}{5}$ be written as a percent?

    a. 40 percent

    b. 125 percent

    c. 90 percent

    d. 80 percent

    e. 85 percent

37. If Danny takes 48 minutes to walk 3 miles, how long should it take him to walk 5 miles maintaining the same speed?

    a. 32 min

    b. 64 min

    c. 80 min

    d. 96 min

    e. 78 min

38. A solution needs 5 ml of saline for every 8 ml of medicine given. How much saline is needed for 45 ml of medicine?

    a. $\frac{225}{8}$ ml

    b. 72 ml

    c. 28 ml

    d. $\frac{45}{8}$ ml

    e. 25 ml

39. If $\frac{5}{2} \div \frac{1}{3} = n$, then n is between:
    a. 5 and 7
    b. 7 and 9
    c. 9 and 11
    d. 3 and 5
    e. 11 and 13

40. Which common denominator would be used in order to evaluate $\frac{2}{3} + \frac{4}{5}$?
    a. 15
    b. 3
    c. 5
    d. 10
    e. 8

41. Which of the following equations best represents the problem below?
The width of a rectangle is 2 centimeters less than the length. If the perimeter of the rectangle is 44 centimeters, then what are the dimensions of the rectangle?

    a. $2l + 2(l - 2) = 44$
    b. $(l + 2) + (l + 2) + l = 48$
    c. $l \times (l - 2) = 44$
    d. $(l + 2) + (l + 2) + l = 44$
    e. $2(l - 2) = 44$

42. A piggy bank contains 12 dollars' worth of nickels. A nickel weighs 5 grams, and the empty piggy bank weighs 1050 grams. What is the total weight of the full piggy bank?
    a. 1,110 grams
    b. 1,200 grams
    c. 2,150 grams
    d. 2,200 grams
    e. 2,250 grams

43. Last year, the New York City area received approximately $27\frac{3}{4}$ inches of snow. The Denver area received approximately 3 times as much snow as New York City. How much snow fell in Denver?

    a. $71\frac{3}{4}$ inches

    b. $27\frac{1}{4}$ inches

    c. $89\frac{1}{4}$ inches

    d. $83\frac{1}{4}$ inches

    e. $86\frac{1}{2}$ inches

44. Which of the following would be an instance in which ordinal numbers are used?
    a. Katie scored a 9 out of 10 on her quiz.
    b. Matthew finished second in the spelling bee.
    c. Jacob missed one day of school last month.
    d. Kim was 5 minutes late to school this morning.
    e. John was on vacation for 6 days.

45. The graph shows the position of a car over a 10-second time interval. Which of the following is the correct interpretation of the graph for the interval 1 to 3 seconds?

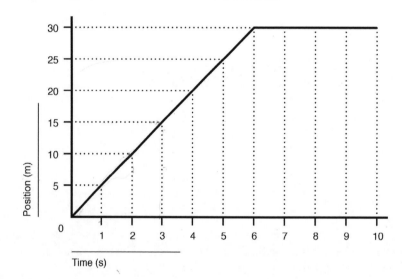

    a. The car remains in the same position.
    b. The car is traveling at a speed of 5m/s.
    c. The car is traveling up a hill.
    d. The car is traveling at 5mph.
    e. The car accelerates at a rate of 5m/s.

46. If Sarah reads at an average rate of 21 pages in four nights, how long will it take her to read 140 pages?
    a. 6 nights
    b. 26 nights
    c. 8 nights
    d. 27 nights
    e. 7 nights

47. The phone bill is calculated each month using the equation $c = 50g + 75$. The cost of the phone bill per month is represented by c, and g represents the gigabytes of data used that month. What is the value and interpretation of the slope of this equation?
    a. 75 dollars per day
    b. 75 gigabytes per day
    c. 50 dollars per day
    d. 50 dollars per gigabyte
    e. 125 dollars per gigabyte

48. How will the following number be written in standard form: $(1 \times 10^4) + (3 \times 10^3) + (7 \times 10^1) + (8 \times 10^0)$
    a. 137
    b. 13,780
    c. 1,378
    d. 8,731
    e. 13,078

49. What is the area of the regular hexagon shown below?

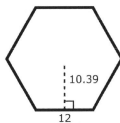

10.39

12

    a. 72
    b. 124.68
    c. 374.04
    d. 748.08
    e. 372.96

50. The area of a given rectangle is 24 centimeters. If the measure of each side is multiplied by 3, what is the area of the new figure?
    a. 48cm
    b. 72cm
    c. 216cm
    d. 13,824cm
    e. 224 cm

Answer Explanations #1

1. A: Compare each numeral after the decimal point to figure out which overall number is greatest. Choices A (1.43785) and C (1.43592) both have the same tenths (4) and hundredths (3). However, the thousandths is greater in answer A (7), so A has the greatest value overall.

2. D: By grouping the four numbers in the answer into factors of the two numbers of the question (6 and 12), it can be determined that (3 x 2) x (4 x 3) = 6 x 12. Alternatively, each of the answer choices could be prime factored or multiplied out and compared to the original value. 6×12 has a value of 72 and a prime factorization of $2^3 \times 3^2$. The answer choices respectively have values of 64, 84, 108, 72, and 144 and prime factorizations of 2^6, $2^2 \times 3 \times 7$, $2^2 \times 3^3$, and $2^3 \times 3^2$, so answer D is the correct choice.

3. C: The sum total percentage of a pie chart must equal 100%. Since the CD sales take up less than half of the chart and more than a quarter (25%), it can be determined to be 40% overall. This can also be measured with a protractor. The angle of a circle is 360°. Since 25% of 360 would be 90° and 50% would be 180°, the angle percentage of CD sales falls in between; therefore, it would be answer C.

4. B: Since $850 is the price *after* a 20% discount, $850 represents 80% of the original price. To determine the original price, set up a proportion with the ratio of the sale price (850) to original price (unknown) equal to the ratio of sale percentage:

$$\frac{850}{x} = \frac{80}{100}$$

(where *x* represents the unknown original price)

To solve a proportion, cross multiply the numerators and denominators and set the products equal to each other: (850)(100) = (80)(x). Multiplying each side results in the equation 85,000=80x.

To solve for *x*, divide both sides by 80: $\frac{85,000}{80} = \frac{80x}{80}$, resulting in x=1062.5. Remember that *x* represents the original price. Subtracting the sale price from the original price ($1062.50-$850) indicates that Frank saved $212.50.

5. E: 85% of a number means that number should be multiplied by 0.85: $0.85 \times 20 = \frac{85}{100} \times \frac{20}{1}$, which can be simplified to $\frac{17}{20} \times \frac{20}{1} = 17$.

6. A: First simplify the larger fraction by separating it into two. When dividing one fraction by another, remember to *invert* the second fraction and multiply the two as follows:

$$\frac{5}{7} \times \frac{11}{9}$$

The resulting fraction $\frac{55}{63}$ cannot be simplified further, so this is the answer to the problem.

7. D: First, subtract $1437 from $2334.50 to find Johnny's monthly savings; this equals $897.50. Then, multiply this amount by 3 to find out how much he will have (in three months) before he pays for his vacation: this equals $2692.50. Finally, subtract the cost of the vacation ($1750) from this amount to find how much Johnny will have left: $942.50.

8. B: Dividing by 98 can be approximated by dividing by 100, which would mean shifting the decimal point of the numerator to the left by 2. The result is 4.2 which rounds to 4.

9. D: To find the average of a set of values, add the values together and then divide by the total number of values. In this case, include the unknown value of what Dwayne needs to score on his next test, in order to solve it.

$$\frac{78 + 92 + 83 + 97 + x}{5} = 90$$

Add the unknown value to the new average total, which is 5. Then multiply each side by 5 to simplify the equation, resulting in:

$$78 + 92 + 83 + 97 + x = 450$$
$$350 + x = 450$$
$$x = 100$$

Dwayne would need to get a perfect score of 100 in order to get an average of at least 90.

Test this answer by substituting back into the original formula.

$$\frac{78 + 92 + 83 + 97 + 100}{5} = 90$$

10. D: For an even number of total values, the *median* is calculated by finding the *mean* or average of the two middle values once all values have been arranged in ascending order from least to greatest. In this case, $(92 + 83) \div 2$ would equal the median 87.5, answer *D*.

11. C: Follow the *order of operations* in order to solve this problem. Solve the parentheses first, and then follow the remainder as usual.

$$(6 \times 4) - 9$$

This equals $24 - 9$ or 15, answer *C*.

12. D: Three girls for every two boys can be expressed as a ratio: 3:2. This can be visualized as splitting the school into 5 groups: 3 girl groups and 2 boy groups. The number of students which are in each group can be found by dividing the total number of students by 5:

650 divided by 5 equals 1 part, or 130 students per group

To find the total number of girls, multiply the number of students per group (130) by how the number of girl groups in the school (3). This equals 390, answer *D*.

13. E: If the average of all six numbers is 6, that means $\frac{a+b+c+d+e+x}{6} = 6$. The sum of the first five numbers is 25, so this equation can be simplified to $\frac{25+x}{6} = 6$. Multiplying both sides by 6 gives $25 + x = 36$, and x, or the sixth number, can be solved to equal 11.

14. C: Kimberley worked 4.5 hours at the rate of $10/h and 1 hour at the rate of $12/h. The problem states that her pay is rounded to the nearest hour, so the 4.5 hours would round up to 5 hours at the rate of $10/h. (5h)($10/h)+(1h)($12/h)= $50+$12= $62.

15. C: The first step is to depict each number using decimals. $\frac{91}{100} = 0.91$

Multiplying both the numerator and denominator of $\frac{4}{5}$ by 20 makes it $\frac{80}{100}$ or 0.80; the closest approximation of $\frac{2}{3}$ would be $\frac{66}{100}$ or 0.66 recurring. Rearrange each expression in ascending order, as found in answer *C*.

16. E: The sample space is made up of $8 + 7 + 6 + 5 = 26$ balls. The probability of pulling each individual ball is $^1/_{26}$. Since there are 7 yellow balls, the probability of pulling a yellow ball is $^7/_{26}$.

17. B: For the first card drawn, the probability of a King being pulled is $^4/_{52}$. Since this card isn't replaced, if a King is drawn first, the probability of a King being drawn second is $^3/_{51}$. The probability of a King being drawn in both the first and second draw is the product of the two probabilities: $^4/_{52}$ x $^3/_{51} = ^{12}/_{2652}$ which, divided by 12, equals $^1/_{221}$.

18. A: To find the fraction of the bill that the first three people pay, the fractions need to be added, which means finding common denominator. The common denominator will be 60. $\frac{1}{5} + \frac{1}{4} + \frac{1}{3} = \frac{12}{60} + \frac{15}{60} + \frac{20}{60} = \frac{47}{60}$. The remainder of the bill is $1 - \frac{47}{60} = \frac{60}{60} - \frac{47}{60} = \frac{13}{60}$.

19. B: Simplify each mixed number of the problem into a fraction by multiplying the denominator by the whole number and adding the numerator:

$$\frac{14}{3} - \frac{31}{9}$$

Since the first denominator is a multiple of the second, simplify it further by multiplying both the numerator and denominator of the first expression by 3 so that the denominators of the fractions are equal.

$$\frac{42}{9} - \frac{31}{9} = \frac{11}{9}$$

Simplifying this further, divide the numerator 11 by the denominator 9; this leaves 1 with a remainder of 2. To write this as a mixed number, place the remainder over the denominator, resulting in $1\frac{2}{9}$.

20. A: The total fraction taken up by green and red shirts will be $\frac{1}{3} + \frac{2}{5} = \frac{5}{15} + \frac{6}{15} = \frac{11}{15}$. The remaining fraction is $1 - \frac{11}{15} = \frac{15}{15} - \frac{11}{15} = \frac{4}{15}$.

21. C: If she has used 1/3 of the paint, she has 2/3 remaining. $2\frac{1}{2}$ gallons are the same as $\frac{5}{2}$ gallons. The calculation is $\frac{2}{3} \times \frac{5}{2} = \frac{5}{3} = 1\frac{2}{3}$ gallons.

22. C: Let *r* be the number of red cans and *b* be the number of blue cans. One equation is $r + b = 10$. The total price is \$16, and the prices for each can means $1r + 2b = 16$. Multiplying the first equation on both sides by -1 results in $-r - b = -10$. Add this equation to the second equation, leaving $b = 6$. So, she bought 6 *blue* cans. From the first equation, this means *r* = 4; thus, she bought 4 *red* cans.

23. C: Janice will be choosing 4 employees out of a set of 6 applicants, so this will be given by the choice function. The following equation shows the choice function worked out:

$$\binom{6}{4} = \frac{6!}{4!\,(6-4)!} = \frac{6!}{4!\,(2)!} = \frac{6 \cdot 5 \cdot 4 \cdot 3 \cdot 2 \cdot 1}{4 \cdot 3 \cdot 2 \cdot 1 \cdot 2 \cdot 1} = \frac{6 \cdot 5}{2} = 15$$

24. D: $\frac{3}{100}$. Each digit to the left of the decimal point represents a higher multiple of 10 and each digit to the right of the decimal point represents a quotient of a higher multiple of 10 for the divisor. The first digit to the right of the decimal point is equal to the value ÷ 10. The second digit to the right of the decimal point is equal to the value ÷ (10 × 10), or the value ÷ 100.

25. E: Using the order of operations, multiplication and division are computed first from left to right. Multiplication is on the left; therefore, the teacher should perform multiplication first.

26. A: 847.90. The hundredth place value is located two digits to the right of the decimal point (the digit 9). The digit to the right of the place value is examined to decide whether to round up or keep the digit. In this case, the digit 6 is 5 or greater so the hundredth place is rounded up. When rounding up, if the digit to be increased is a 9, the digit to its left is increased by one and the digit in the desired place value is made a zero. Therefore, the number is rounded to 847.90.

27. C: Perimeter is found by calculating the sum of all sides of the polygon. $9 + 9 + 9 + 8 + 8 + s = 56$, where s is the missing side length. Therefore, 43 plus the missing side length is equal to 56. The missing side length is 13 cm.

28. A: $16\frac{1}{2}$. A mixed number contains both a whole number and either a fraction or a decimal. Therefore, the mixed number is $16\frac{1}{2}$.

29. A: The place value to the right of the thousandth place, which would be the ten-thousandth place, is what gets utilized. The value in the thousandth place is 7. The number in the place value to its right is greater than 4, so the 7 gets bumped up to 8. Everything to its right turns to a zero, to get 245.2680. The zero is dropped because it is part of the decimal.

30. C: To solve for the value of b, both sides of the equation need to be equalized.

Start by cancelling out the lower value of -4 by adding 4 to both sides:

$5b - 4 = 2b + 17$
$5b - 4 + 4 = 2b + 17 + 4$
$5b = 2b + 21$

The variable b is the same on each side, so subtract the lower 2b from each side:

$5b = 2b + 21$
$5b - 2b = 2b + 21 - 2b$
$3b = 21$

Then divide both sides by 3 to get the value of *b*:

$$3b = 21$$

$$\frac{3b}{3} = \frac{21}{3}$$

$$b = 7$$

31. C: The first step in solving this problem is expressing the result in fraction form. Separate this problem first by solving the division operation of the last two fractions. When dividing one fraction by another, invert or flip the second fraction and then multiply the numerator and denominator.

$$\frac{7}{10} \times \frac{2}{1} = \frac{14}{10}$$

Next, multiply the first fraction with this value:

$$\frac{3}{5} \times \frac{14}{10} = \frac{42}{50}$$

Decimals are expressions of 1 or 100%, so multiply both the numerator and denominator by 2 to get the fraction as an expression of 100.

$$\frac{42}{50} \times \frac{2}{2} = \frac{84}{100}$$

In decimal form, this would be expressed as 0.84.

32. B: 100 cm is equal to 1 m. 1.3 divided by 100 is 0.013. Therefore, 1.3 cm is equal to 0.013 mm. Because 1 cm is equal to 10 mm, 1.3 cm is equal to 13 mm.

33. C: $\frac{1}{3}$ of the shirts sold were patterned. Therefore, $1 - \frac{1}{3} = \frac{2}{3}$ of the shirts sold were solid. Anytime "of" a quantity appears in a word problem, multiplication needs to be used. Therefore, $192 \times \frac{2}{3} = 192 \times \frac{2}{3} = \frac{384}{3} = 128$ solid shirts were sold. The entire expression is $192 \times \left(1 - \frac{1}{3}\right)$.

34. B: A rectangle is a specific type of parallelogram. It has 4 right angles. A square is a rhombus that has 4 right angles. Therefore, a square is always a rectangle because it has two sets of parallel lines and 4 right angles.

35. D: Area = length x width. The answer must be in square inches, so all values must be converted to inches. $\frac{1}{2}$ ft is equal to 6 inches. Therefore, the area of the rectangle is equal to $6 \times \frac{11}{2} = \frac{66}{2} = 33$ square inches.

36. D: 80 percent. To convert a fraction to a percent, the fraction is first converted to a decimal. To do so, the numerator is divided by the denominator: $4 \div 5 = 0.8$. To convert a decimal to a percent, the number is multiplied by 100: $0.8 \times 10 = 80\%$.

37. C: 80 min. To solve the problem, a proportion is written consisting of ratios comparing distance and time. One way to set up the proportion is: $\frac{3}{48} = \frac{5}{x} \left(\frac{distance}{time} = \frac{distance}{time}\right)$ where *x* represents the unknown value of time. To solve a proportion, the ratios are cross-multiplied: $(3)(x) = (5)(48) \rightarrow 3x = 240$. The equation is solved by isolating the variable, or dividing by 3 on both sides, to produce $x = 80$.

38. A: Every 8 ml of medicine requires 5 ml. The 45 ml first needs to be split into portions of 8 ml. This results in $\frac{45}{8}$ portions. Each portion requires 5 ml. Therefore, $\frac{45}{8} \times 5 = 45 \times \frac{5}{8} = \frac{225}{8}$ ml is necessary.

39. B: $\frac{5}{2} \div \frac{1}{3} = \frac{5}{2} \times \frac{3}{1} = \frac{15}{2} = 7.5$.

40. A: A common denominator must be found. The least common denominator is 15 because it has both 5 and 3 as factors. The fractions must be rewritten using 15 as the denominator.

41. A: The first step is to determine the unknown, which is in terms of the length, l.

The second step is to translate the problem into the equation using the perimeter of a rectangle, $P = 2l + 2w$. The width is the length minus 2 centimeters. The resulting equation is $2l + 2(l - 2) = 44$. The equation can be solved as follows:

$2l + 2l - 4 = 44$	Apply the distributive property on the left side of the equation
$4l - 4 = 44$	Combine like terms on the left side of the equation
$4l = 48$	Add 4 to both sides of the equation
$l = 12$	Divide both sides of the equation by 4

The length of the rectangle is 12 centimeters. The width is the length minus 2 centimeters, which is 10 centimeters. Checking the answers for length and width forms the following equation:

$$44 = 2(12) + 2(10)$$

The equation can be solved using the order of operations to form a true statement: $44 = 44$.

42. E: A dollar contains 20 nickels. Therefore, if there are 12 dollars' worth of nickels, there are $12 \times 20 = 240$ nickels. Each nickel weighs 5 grams. Therefore, the weight of the nickels is $240 \times 5 = 1{,}200$ grams. Adding in the weight of the empty piggy bank, the filled bank weighs 2,250 grams.

43. D: 3 must be multiplied times $27\frac{3}{4}$. In order to easily do this, the mixed number should be converted into an improper fraction. $27\frac{3}{4} = 27 \times 4 + \frac{3}{4} = \frac{111}{4}$. Therefore, Denver had approximately $3 \times \frac{111}{4} = \frac{333}{4}$ inches of snow. The improper fraction can be converted back into a mixed number through division. $\frac{333}{4} = 83\frac{1}{4}$ inches.

44. B: Ordinal numbers represent a ranking. Placing second in a competition is a ranking among the other participants of the spelling bee.

45. B: The car is traveling at a speed of five meters per second. On the interval from one to three seconds, the position changes by fifteen meters. By making this change in position over time into a rate, the speed becomes ten meters in two seconds or five meters in one second.

46. D: This problem can be solved by setting up a proportion involving the given information and the unknown value. The proportion is $\frac{21\ pages}{4\ nights} = \frac{140\ pages}{x\ nigh}$. Solving the proportion by cross-multiplying, the equation becomes $21x = 4 * 140$, where $x = 26.67$. Since it is not an exact number of nights, the answer is rounded up to 27 nights. Twenty-six nights would not give Sarah enough time.

47. D: The slope from this equation is 50, and it is interpreted as the cost per gigabyte used. Since the g-value represents number of gigabytes and the equation is set equal to the cost in dollars, the slope relates these two values. For every gigabyte used on the phone, the bill goes up 50 dollars.

48. E: 13,078. The power of 10 by which a digit is multiplied corresponds with the number of zeros following the digit when expressing its value in standard form. Therefore, $(1 \times 10^4) + (3 \times 10^3) + (7 \times 10^1) + (8 \times 10^0) = 10,000 + 3,000 + 70 + 8 = 13,078$.

49. C: 374.04. The formula for finding the area of a regular polygon is $A = \frac{1}{2} \times a \times P$ where a is the length of the apothem (from the center to any side at a right angle) and P is the perimeter of the figure. The apothem a is given as 10.39 and the perimeter can be found by multiplying the length of one side by the number of sides (since the polygon is regular): $P = 12 \times 6 \rightarrow P = 72$. To find the area, substitute the values for a and P into the formula $A = \frac{1}{2} \times a \times P \rightarrow A = \frac{1}{2} \times (10.39) \times (72) \rightarrow A = 374.04$.

50. C: 216cm. Because area is a two-dimensional measurement, the dimensions are multiplied by a scale that is squared to determine the scale of the corresponding areas. The dimensions of the rectangle are multiplied by a scale of 3. Therefore, the area is multiplied by a scale of 3^2 (which is equal to 9): $24cm \times 9 = 216cm$.

CBEST Math Practice Test #2

1. At the beginning of the day, Xavier has 20 apples. At lunch, he meets his sister Emma and gives her half of his apples. After lunch, he stops by his neighbor Jim's house and gives him 6 of his apples. He then uses ¾ of his remaining apples to make an apple pie for dessert at dinner. At the end of the day, how many apples does Xavier have left?

    a. 4
    b. 6
    c. 2
    d. 1
    e. 3

2. What is the product of two irrational numbers?

    a. Irrational
    b. Rational
    c. Irrational or rational
    d. Complex and imaginary
    e. Imaginary

3. Being as specific as possible, how is the number -4 classified?

    a. Real, rational, integer, whole, natural
    b. Real, rational, integer, natural
    c. Real, rational, integer
    d. Real, irrational, complex
    e. Real, irrational, whole

4. $4\frac{1}{3} + 3\frac{3}{4} =$

    a. $6\frac{5}{12}$
    b. $8\frac{1}{12}$
    c. $8\frac{2}{3}$
    d. $7\frac{7}{12}$
    e. $7\frac{4}{12}$

5. What is the perimeter of the figure below? Note that the solid outer line is the perimeter.

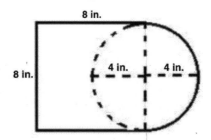

a. 48.565 in
b. 36.565 in
c. 39.78 in
d. 39.565 in
e. 41.12 in

6. Alan currently weighs 200 pounds, but he wants to lose weight to get down to 175 pounds. What is this difference in kilograms? (1 pound is approximately equal to 0.45 kilograms.)
   a. 9 kg
   b. 11.25 kg
   c. 78.75 kg
   d. 90 kg
   e. 25 kg

7. Mom's car drove 72 miles in 90 minutes. How fast did she drive in feet per second?
   a. 0.8 feet per second
   b. 48.9 feet per second
   c. 0.009 feet per second
   d. 70.4 feet per second
   e. 21.3 feet per second

8. Solve $V = lwh$ for h.
   a. $lwV = h$
   b. $h = \dfrac{V}{lw}$
   c. $h = \dfrac{Vl}{w}$
   d. $h = \dfrac{Vw}{l}$
   e. $h = \dfrac{Vl}{w}$

9. If $\sqrt{1 + x} = 4$, what is x?
   a. 10
   b. 15
   c. 20
   d. 25
   e. 36

10. Twenty is 40% of what number?

    a. 60

    b. 8

    c. 200

    d. 70

    e. 50

11. What is the simplified form of the expression $1.2 * 10^{12} \div 3.0 * 10^8$?

    a. $0.4 * 10^4$

    b. $4.0 * 10^4$

    c. $4.0 * 10^3$

    d. $3.6 * 10^{20}$

    e. $4.0 * 10^2$

12. You measure the width of your door to be 36 inches. The true width of the door is 35.75 inches. What is the relative error in your measurement?

    a. 0.7%

    b. 0.007%

    c. 0.99%

    d. 0.1%

    e. 7.0%

13. What are the y-intercept(s) for $y = x^2 + 3x - 4$?

    a. $y = 1$

    b. $y = -4$

    c. $y = 3$

    d. $y = 4$

    e. $y = -3$

14. A six-sided die is rolled. What is the probability that the roll is 1 or 2?

    a. $\frac{1}{6}$

    b. $\frac{1}{4}$

    c. $\frac{1}{3}$

    d. $\frac{1}{2}$

    e. $\frac{1}{36}$

15. A line passes through the origin and through the point (-3, 4). What is the slope of the line?

    a. $-\frac{4}{3}$

    b. $-\frac{3}{4}$

    c. $\frac{4}{3}$

    d. $\frac{3}{4}$

    e. $\frac{1}{3}$

16. Keith's bakery had 252 customers go through its doors last week. This week, that number increased to 378. Express this increase as a percentage.

    a. 26%

    b. 50%

    c. 35%

    d. 12%

    e. 28%

17. The following graph compares the various test scores of the top three students in each of these teacher's classes. Based on the graph, which teacher's students had the lowest range of test scores?

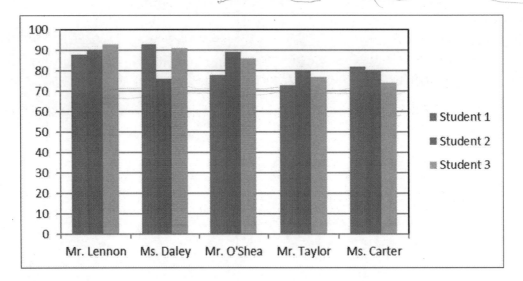

    a. Mr. Lennon

    b. Mr. O'Shea

    c. Mr. Taylor

    d. Ms. Daley

    e. Ms. Carter

18. What's the probability of rolling a 6 at least once in two rolls of a die?

    a. $^1/_3$

    b. $^1/_{36}$

    c. $^1/_6$

    d. $^1/_{12}$

    e. $^{11}/_{36}$

19. Given the set $A = \{1, 2, 3, 4, 5, 6, 7, 8, 9, 10\}$ and $B = \{1, 2, 3, 4, 5\}$, what is $A - (A \cap B)$?

    a. $\{6, 7, 8, 9, 10\}$

    b. $\{1, 2, 3, 4, 5\}$

    c. $\{1, 2, 3, 4, 5, 6, 7, 8, 9, 10\}$

    d. $\emptyset$

    e. $\{-1, -2, -3, -4, -5\}$

20. An equilateral triangle has a perimeter of 18 feet. If a square whose sides have the same length as one side of the triangle is built, what will be the area of the square?

    a. 6 square feet

    b. 36 square feet

    c. 256 square feet

    d. 1000 square feet

    e. 324 square feet

21. In a group of 20 men, the median weight is 180 pounds and the range is 30 pounds. If each man gains 10 pounds, which of the following would be true?

    a. The median weight will increase, and the range will remain the same.

    b. The median weight and range will both remain the same.

    c. The median weight will stay the same, and the range will increase.

    d. The median weight and range will both increase.

    e. The median weight will increase, and the range will decrease.

22. For the following similar triangles, what are the values of x and y (rounded to one decimal place)?

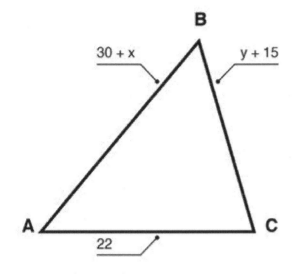
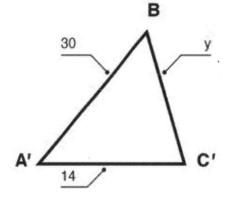

    a. $x = 16.5, y = 25.1$

    b. $x = 19.5, y = 24.1$

    c. $x = 17.1, y = 26.3$

    d. $x = 26.3, y = 17.1$

    e. $x = 24.1, y = 19.5$

23. On Monday, Robert mopped the floor in 4 hours. On Tuesday, he did it in 3 hours. If on Monday, his average rate of mopping was p sq. ft. per hour, what was his average rate on Tuesday?

    a. $\frac{4}{3}p$ sq. ft. per hour

    b. $\frac{3}{4}p$ sq. ft. per hour

    c. $\frac{5}{4}p$ sq. ft. per hour

    d. $p + 1$ sq. ft. per hour

    e. $\frac{1}{3}p$ sq. ft. per hour

24. Which of the following inequalities is equivalent to $3 - \frac{1}{2}x \geq 2$?

    a. $x \geq 2$
    b. $x \leq 2$
    c. $x \geq 1$
    d. $x \leq 1$
    e. $x \leq -2$

25. For which of the following are $x = 4$ and $x = -4$ solutions?

    a. $x^2 + 16 = 0$
    b. $x^2 + 4x - 4 = 0$
    c. $x^2 - 2x - 2 = 0$
    d. $x^2 - x - 16 = 0$
    e. $x^2 - 16 = 0$

26. Ten students take a test. Five students get a 50. Four students get a 70. If the average score is 55, what was the last student's score?

    a. 20
    b. 40
    c. 50
    d. 60
    e. 62

27. A sample data set contains the following values: 1, 3, 5, 7. What's the standard deviation of the set?

    a. 2.58
    b. 4
    c. 6.23
    d. 1.1
    e. 0.25

28. A company invests $50,000 in a building where they can produce saws. If the cost of producing one saw is $40, then which function expresses the amount of money the company pays? The variable y is the money paid and x is the number of saws produced.

    a. $y = 50{,}000x + 40$
    b. $y + 40 = x - 50{,}000$
    c. $y = 40x - 50{,}000$
    d. $y = 40x + 50{,}000$
    e. $y = 4x + 50{,}000$

29. A pair of dice is thrown, and the sum of the two scores is calculated. What's the expected value of the roll?

    a. 5
    b. 6
    c. 7
    d. 8
    e. 9

30. A line passes through the point (1, 2) and crosses the y-axis at $y = 1$. Which of the following is an equation for this line?

    a. $y = 2x$
    b. $y = x + 1$
    c. $x + y = 1$
    d. $y = \frac{x}{2} - 2$
    e. $y = x - 1$

31. What is the solution to $4 \times 7 + (25 - 21)^2 \div 2$?

    a. 512
    b. 36
    c. 60.5
    d. 22
    e. 16

32. What is the solution to $(2 \times 20) \div (7 + 1) + (6 \times 0.01) + (4 \times 0.001)$?
    a. 5.064
    b. 5.64
    c. 5.0064
    d. 48.064
    e. 56.4

33. In a school with 300 students, there are 10 students with red hair, 50 students with black hair, 180 students with brown hair, and 60 students with blonde hair. What is the ratio of blonde hair to brown hair?
    a. 3:1
    b. 2:1
    c. 1:3
    d. 1:2
    e. 1:5

34. What is the value of the sum of $\frac{1}{3}$ and $\frac{2}{5}$?

    a. $\frac{3}{8}$

    b. $\frac{11}{15}$

    c. $\frac{11}{30}$

    d. $\frac{4}{5}$

    e. $\frac{2}{8}$

35. Divide and reduce 4/13 ÷ 27/169.

  a. 52/27

  b. 51/27

  c. 52/29

  d. 51/29

  e. 7/13

36. 6 is 30% of what number?

  a. 18

  b. 20

  c. 24

  d. 25

  e. 26

37. $3\frac{2}{3} - 1\frac{4}{5} =$

  a. $1\frac{13}{15}$

  b. $\frac{14}{15}$

  c. $2\frac{2}{3}$

  d. $\frac{4}{5}$

  e. $\frac{4}{15}$

38. A pizzeria owner regularly creates jumbo pizzas, each with a radius of 9 inches. She is mathematically inclined, and wants to know the area of the pizza to purchase the correct boxes and know how much she is feeding her customers. What is the area of the circle, in terms of π, with a radius of 9 inches?

  a. 3π in²

  b. 18π in²

  c. 90π in²

  d. 9π in²

  e. 81π in²

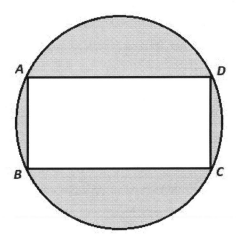

39. Rectangle *ABCD* is inscribed in the circle above. The length of side *AB* is 9 inches and the length of side *BC* is 12 inches. What is the area of the shaded region?
    a. 64.4 sq. in.
    b. 68.6 sq. in.
    c. 62.8 sq. in.
    d. 61.3 sq. in.
    e. 64.6 sq. in.

40. Using the following diagram, calculate the total circumference, rounding to the nearest decimal place:

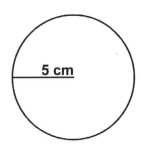

    a. 25.0 cm
    b. 15.7 cm
    c. 78.5 cm
    d. 50.0 cm
    e. 31.4 cm

41. What is the probability of randomly picking the winner and runner-up from a race of 4 horses and distinguishing which is the winner?
    a. $\frac{1}{4}$

    b. $\frac{1}{2}$

    c. $\frac{1}{16}$

    d. $\frac{1}{12}$

    e. $\frac{1}{64}$

42. Which is closest to 17.8 × 9.9?
    a. 140
    b. 180
    c. 200
    d. 350
    e. 400

$$G = .035O + .26$$

43. The linear regression model above is based on an analysis of the price of a gallon of gas (G) at 15 gas stations compared to the price of a barrel of oil (O) at the time. Based on this model, which of the following statements are true?
    I. There is a negative correlation between G and O.
    II. When oil is $55 per barrel then gas is approximately $2.19 per gallon.
    III. The slope of the line indicates that as O increases by 1, G increases by .035.
    IV. If the price of oil increases by $8 per barrel then the price of gas will increase by approximately $0.18 per gallon.
    a. I and II
    b. II only
    c. II and III
    d. I and III
    e. II, III, and IV

44. Given the value of a given stock at monthly intervals, which graph should be used to best represent the trend of the stock?
    a. Box plot
    b. Line plot
    c. Line graph
    d. Circle graph
    e. Dot plot

45. The width of a rectangular house is 22 feet. What is the perimeter of this house if it has the same area as a house that is 33 feet wide and 50 feet long?
    a. 184 feet
    b. 200 feet
    c. 192 feet
    d. 206 feet
    e. 194 feet

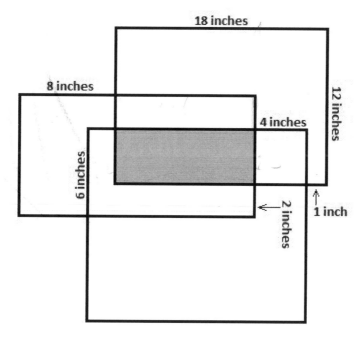

46. In the figure above, what is the area of the shaded region?
    a. 48 sq. inches
    b. 52 sq. inches
    c. 44 sq. inches
    d. 56 sq. inches
    e. 46 sq. inches

47. If $3x = 6y = -2z = 24$, then what does $4xy + z$ equal?
    a. 116
    b. 130
    c. 84
    d. 108
    e. 98

48. $\frac{3}{25} =$
    a. 0.15
    b. 0.1
    c. 0.9
    d. 0.12
    e. 0.19

49. Which of the following is largest?
    a. 0.45
    b. 0.096
    c. 0.3
    d. 0.313
    e. 0.299

50. Which of the following is NOT a way to write 40 percent of N?

    a. $(0.4)N$

    b. $\frac{2}{5}N$

    c. $N \times 0.4$

    d. $\frac{4N}{10}$

    e. $40N$

Answer Explanations #2

1. D: This problem can be solved using basic arithmetic. Xavier starts with 20 apples, then gives his sister half, so 20 divided by 2.

$$\frac{20}{2} = 10$$

He then gives his neighbor 6, so 6 is subtracted from 10.

$$10 - 6 = 4$$

Lastly, he uses ¾ of his apples to make an apple pie, so to find remaining apples, the first step is to subtract ¾ from one and then multiply the difference by 4.

$$\left(1 - \frac{3}{4}\right) \times 4 = ?$$

$$\left(\frac{4}{4} - \frac{3}{4}\right) \times 4 = ?$$

$$\left(\frac{1}{4}\right) \times 4 = 1$$

2. C: The product of two irrational numbers can be rational or irrational. Sometimes, the irrational parts of the two numbers cancel each other out, leaving a rational number. For example, $\sqrt{2} * \sqrt{2} = 2$ because the roots cancel each other out. Technically, the product of two irrational numbers can be complex because complex numbers can have either the real or imaginary part (in this case, the imaginary part) equal zero and still be considered a complex number. However, Choice *D* is incorrect because the product of two irrational numbers is not an imaginary number so saying the product is complex *and* imaginary is incorrect.

3. C: The number negative four is classified as a real number because it exists and is not imaginary. It is rational because it does not have a decimal that never ends. It is an integer because it does not have a fractional component. The next classification would be whole numbers, for which negative four does not qualify because it is negative. Although -4 could technically be considered a complex number because complex numbers can have either the real or imaginary part equal zero and still be considered a complex number, Choice *D* is wrong because -4 is not considered an irrational number because it does not have a never-ending decimal component.

4. B: $4\frac{1}{3} + 3\frac{3}{4} = 4 + 3 + \frac{1}{3} + \frac{3}{4} = 7 + \frac{1}{3} + \frac{3}{4}$. Adding the fractions gives $\frac{1}{3} + \frac{3}{4} = \frac{4}{12} + \frac{9}{12} = \frac{13}{12} = 1 + \frac{1}{12}$. Thus, $7 + \frac{1}{3} + \frac{3}{4} = 7 + 1 + \frac{1}{12} = 8\frac{1}{12}$.

5. B: The figure is composed of three sides of a square and a semicircle. The sides of the square are simply added: 8 + 8 + 8 = 24 inches. The circumference of a circle is found by the equation C = 2πr. The radius is 4 in, so the circumference of the circle is 25.13 in. Only half of the circle makes up the outer border of the figure (part of the perimeter) so half of 25.13 in is 12.565 in. Therefore, the total perimeter is: 24 in + 12.565 in = 36.565 in. The other answer choices use the incorrect formula or fail to include all of the necessary sides.

6. B: Using the conversion rate, multiply the projected weight loss of 25 lb by 0.45 $\frac{kg}{lb}$ to get the amount in kilograms (11.25 kg).

7. D: This problem can be solved by using unit conversion. The initial units are miles per minute. The final units need to be feet per second. Converting miles to feet uses the equivalence statement 1 mile = 5,280 feet. Converting minutes to seconds uses the equivalence statement 1 minute = 60 seconds. Setting up the ratios to convert the units is shown in the following equation $\frac{72\ miles}{90\ minutes} * \frac{1\ minute}{60\ seconds} *$ $\frac{5280\ feet}{1\ mile} = 70.4$ feet per second. The initial units cancel out, and the new units are left.

8. B: The formula can be manipulated by dividing both the length, *l*, and the width, *w*, on both sides. The length and width will cancel on the right, leaving height by itself.

9. B: Start by squaring both sides to get $1 + x = 16$. Then subtract 1 from both sides to get $x = 15$.

10. E: Setting up a proportion is the easiest way to represent this situation. The proportion becomes $\frac{20}{x} = \frac{40}{100}$, where cross-multiplication can be used to solve for x. The answer can also be found by observing the two fractions as equivalent, knowing that twenty is half of forty, and fifty is half of one-hundred.

11. C: Division with scientific notation can be solved by grouping the first terms together and grouping the tens together. The first terms can be divided, and the tens terms can be simplified using the rules for exponents. The initial expression becomes $0.4 * 10^4$. This is not in scientific notation because the first number is not between 1 and 10. Shifting the decimal and subtracting one from the exponent yields $4.0 * 10^3$.

12. A: The relative error can be found by finding the absolute error and making it a percent of the true value. The absolute error is $36 - 35.75 = 0.25$. This error is then divided by 36—the true value—to find 0.7%.

13. B: The y-intercept of an equation is found where the x-value is zero. Plugging zero into the equation for x allows the first two terms to cancel out, leaving -4.

14. C: A die has an equal chance for each outcome. Since it has six sides, each outcome has a probability of $\frac{1}{6}$. The chance of a 1 or a 2 is therefore $\frac{1}{6} + \frac{1}{6} = \frac{1}{3}$.

15. A: The slope is given by $m = \frac{y_2 - y_1}{x_2 - x_1} = \frac{0-4}{0-(-3)} = -\frac{4}{3}$.

16. B: First, calculate the difference between the larger value and the smaller value.

378 − 252 = 126

17. A: To calculate the range in a set of data, subtract the highest value with the lowest value. In this graph, the range of Mr. Lennon's students is 5, which can be seen physically in the graph as having the smallest difference compared with the other teachers between the highest value and the lowest value.

18. E: The addition rule is necessary to determine the probability because a 6 can be rolled on either roll of the die. The rule used is $P(A \text{ or } B) = P(A) + P(B) - P(A \text{ and } B)$. The probability of a 6 being individually rolled is $1/6$ and the probability of a 6 being rolled twice is $1/6 \cdot 1/6 = 1/36$. Therefore, the probability that a 6 is rolled at least once is $1/6 + 1/6 - 1/36 = 11/36$

19. A: $(A \cap B)$ is equal to the intersection of the two sets A and B, which is $\{1, 2, 3, 4, 5\}$. $A - (A \cap B)$ is equal to the elements of A that are *not* included in the set $(A \cap B)$. Therefore, $A - (A \cap B) = \{6, 7, 8, 9, 10\}$.

20. B: An equilateral triangle has three sides of equal length, so if the total perimeter is 18 feet, each side must be 6 feet long. A square with sides of 6 feet will have an area of $6^2 = 36$ square feet.

21. A: If each man gains 10 pounds, every original data point will increase by 10 pounds. Therefore, the man with the original median will still have the median value, but that value will increase by 10. The smallest value and largest value will also increase by 10 and, therefore, the difference between the two won't change. The range does not change in value and, thus, remains the same.

22. C: Because the triangles are similar, the lengths of the corresponding sides are proportional. Therefore, $\frac{30+x}{30} = \frac{22}{14} = \frac{y+15}{y}$. This results in the equation $14(30 + x) = 22 \cdot 30$ which, when solved, gives $x = 17.1$. The proportion also results in the equation $14(y + 15) = 22y$, which, when solved, gives $y = 26.3$.

23. A: Robert accomplished his task on Tuesday in ¾ the time compared to Monday. He must have worked 4/3 as fast.

24. B: To simplify this inequality, subtract 3 from both sides to get $-\frac{1}{2}x \geq -1$. Then, multiply both sides by -2 (remembering this flips the direction of the inequality) to get $x \leq 2$.

25. E: There are two ways to approach this problem. Each value can be substituted into each equation. Choice *A* can be eliminated, since $4^2 + 16 = 32$. Choice *B* can be eliminated, since $4^2 + 4 \cdot 4 - 4 = 28$. Choice *C* can be eliminated, since $4^2 - 2 \cdot 4 - 2 = 6$. But, plugging in either value into $x^2 - 16$ gives $(\pm 4)^2 - 16 = 16 - 16 = 0$.

26. A: Let the unknown score be x. The average will be $\frac{5 \cdot 50 + 4 \cdot 70 + x}{10} = \frac{530+x}{10} = 55$. Multiply both sides by 10 to get $530 + x = 550$, or $x = 20$.

27. A: First, the sample mean must be calculated. $\bar{x} = \frac{1}{4}(1 + 3 + 5 + 7) = 4$. The standard deviation of the data set is:

$$\sigma = \sqrt{\frac{\sum(x - \bar{x})^2}{n - 1}}$$

$n = 4$ represents the number of data points. Therefore:

$$\sigma = \sqrt{\frac{1}{3}[(1 - 4)^2 + (3 - 4)^2 + (5 - 4)^2 + (7 - 4)^2]} = \sqrt{\frac{1}{3}(9 + 1 + 1 + 9)} = 2.58$$

28. D: For manufacturing costs, there is a linear relationship between the cost to the company and the number produced, with a *y*-intercept given by the base cost of acquiring the means of production, and a slope given by the cost to produce one unit. In this case, that base cost is \$50,000, while the cost per unit is \$40. So, $y = 40x + 50,000$.

29. C: The expected value is equal to the total sum of each product of individual score and probability. There are 36 possible rolls. The probability of rolling a 2 is $\frac{1}{36}$. The probability of rolling a 3 is $\frac{2}{36}$. The probability of rolling a 4 is $\frac{3}{36}$. The probability of rolling a 5 is $\frac{4}{36}$. The probability of rolling a 6 is $\frac{5}{36}$. The probability of rolling a 7 is $\frac{6}{36}$. The probability of rolling an 8 is $\frac{5}{36}$. The probability of rolling a 9 is $\frac{4}{36}$. The probability of rolling a 10 is $\frac{3}{36}$. The probability of rolling an 11 is $\frac{2}{36}$. Finally, the probability of rolling a 12 is $\frac{1}{36}$.

Each possible outcome is multiplied by the probability of it occurring. Like this:

$$2 \times \frac{1}{36} = a$$

$$3 \times \frac{2}{36} = b$$

$$4 \times \frac{3}{36} = c$$

And so forth.

Then all of those results are added together:

$$a + b + c \ldots = expected\ value$$

In this case, it equals 7.

30. B: From the slope-intercept form, $y = mx + b$, it is known that b is the y-intercept, which is 1. Compute the slope as $\frac{2-1}{1-0} = 1$, so the equation should be $y = x + 1$.

31. B: To solve this correctly, keep in mind the order of operations with the mnemonic PEMDAS (Please Excuse My Dear Aunt Sally). This stands for Parentheses, Exponents, Multiplication, Division, Addition, Subtraction. Taking it step by step, solve the parentheses first:

$4 \times 7 + (4)^2 \div 2$

Then, apply the exponent:

$4 \times 7 + 16 \div 2$

Multiplication and division are both performed next:

$28 + 8 = 36$

32. A: Operations within the parentheses must be completed first. Then, division is completed. Finally, addition is the last operation to complete. When adding decimals, digits within each place value are added together. Therefore, the expression is evaluated as $(2 \times 20) \div (7 + 1) + (6 \times 0.01) + (4 \times 0.001) = 40 \div 8 + 0.06 + 0.004 = 5 + 0.06 + 0.004 = 5.064$.

33. C: There are 60 students with blonde hair and 180 students with brown hair. The ratio would be set up as blonde:brown, so 60:180. When reduced this is 1:3. This means that for every 1 student with blonde hair, there are 3 with brown hair.

34. B: $\frac{11}{15}$. Fractions must have like denominators to be added. The least common multiple of the denominators 3 and 5 is found. The LCM is 15, so both fractions should be changed to equivalent fractions with a denominator of 15. To determine the numerator of the new fraction, the old numerator is multiplied by the same number by which the old denominator is multiplied to obtain the new denominator. For the fraction $\frac{1}{3}$, 3 multiplied by 5 will produce 15. Therefore, the numerator is multiplied by 5 to produce the new numerator $\left(\frac{1\times5}{3\times5}=\frac{5}{15}\right)$. For the fraction $\frac{2}{5}$, multiplying both the numerator and denominator by 3 produces $\frac{6}{15}$. When fractions have like denominators, they are added by adding the numerators and keeping the denominator the same: $\frac{5}{15}+\frac{6}{15}=\frac{11}{15}$.

35. A: 52/27. Set up the division problem.

$$\frac{4}{13} \div \frac{27}{169}$$

Flip the second fraction and multiply.

$$\frac{4}{13} \times \frac{169}{27}$$

Simplify and reduce with cross multiplication.

$$\frac{4}{1} \times \frac{13}{27}$$

Multiply across the top and across the bottom to solve.

$$\frac{4 \times 13}{1 \times 27} = \frac{52}{27}$$

36. B: 30% is 3/10. The number itself must be 10/3 of 6, or $\frac{10}{3} \times 6 = 10 \times 2 = 20$.

37. A: These numbers first need to be changed to improper fractions: $\frac{11}{3} - \frac{9}{5}$. Take 15 as a common denominator: $\frac{11}{3} - \frac{9}{5} =: \frac{55}{15} - \frac{27}{15} = \frac{28}{15} = 1\frac{13}{15}$ (when rewritten to get rid of the partial fraction).

38. E: The formula for the area of the circle is πr^2 and 9 squared is 81. Choice *A* is not the correct answer because that takes the square root of the radius instead of squaring the radius. Choice *B* is not the correct answer because that is 2×9. Choice *C* is not the correct answer because that is 9×10. Choice *D* is not the correct answer because that is simply the value of the radius.

39. B: The inscribed rectangle is 9 X 12 inches. First find the length of *AC* using the Pythagorean Theorem. So, $9^2 + 12^2 = c^2$, where *c* is the length of *AC* in this case. This means that *AC* = 15 inches. This means the diameter of the circle is 15 inches. This can be used to find the area of the entire circle. The formula is πr^2. So, $3.14(7.5)^2 = 176.6$ sq. inches. Then take the area of the rectangle away to find just the area of the shaded region. This is $176.6 - 108 = 68.6$.

40. E: To calculate the circumference of a circle, use the formula $2\pi r$, where r equals the radius or half of the diameter of the circle and $\pi = 3.14\ldots$. Substitute the given information, $2\pi 5 = 31.4\ldots$, answer E.

41. D: The probability of picking the winner of the race is $\frac{1}{4}\left(\frac{number\ of\ favorable\ outcomes}{number\ of\ total\ outcomes}\right)$. Assuming the winner was picked on the first selection, three horses remain from which to choose the runner-up (these are dependent events). Therefore, the probability of picking the runner-up is $\frac{1}{3}$. To determine the probability of multiple events, the probability of each event is multiplied: $\frac{1}{4} \times \frac{1}{3} = \frac{1}{12}$.

42. B: Instead of multiplying these out, the product can be estimated by using $18 \times 10 = 180$. The error here should be lower than 15, since it is rounded to the nearest integer, and the numbers add to something less than 30.

43. C: II and III are the only true statements. If graphed this line would have a positive correlation, which make statement I false. Also, if the price of oil increases by \$8 per barrel then gas price would increase by $.035(8) = \$0.28$ per gallon. This make statement IV false as well.

44. C: The scenario involves data consisting of two variables: month and stock value. Box plots display data consisting of values for one variable. Therefore, a box plot is not an appropriate choice. Both line plots (which are also called dot plots) and circle graphs are used to display frequencies within categorical data. Neither can be used for the given scenario. Line graphs display two numerical variables on a coordinate grid and show trends among the variables, so this is the correct choice.

45. E: First, find the area of the second house. The area is $A = l\,x\,w = 33 \times 50 = 1,650$ square feet. Then use the area formula to determine what length gives the first house an area of 1,650 square feet. So, $1,650 = 22 \times l, l = \frac{1,650}{22} = 75$ feet. Then, use the formula for perimeter to get $75 + 75 + 22 + 22 = 194$ feet.

46. B: This can be determined by finding the length and width of the shaded region. The length can be found using the length of the top rectangle which is 18 inches, then subtracting the extra length of 4 inches and 1 inch. This means the length of the shaded region is 13 inches. Next, the width can be determined using the 6 inch measurement and subtracting the 2 inch measurement. This means that the width is 4 inches. Thus, the area is $13 \times 4 = 52$ sq. inches.

47. A: First solve for x, y, and z. So, $3x = 24, x = 8, 6y = 24, y = 4$, and $-2z = 24, z = -12$. This means the equation would be $4(8)(4) + (-12)$, which equals 116.

48. D: The fraction is converted so that the denominator is 100 by multiplying the numerator and denominator by 4, to get $\frac{3}{25} = \frac{12}{100}$. Dividing a number by 100 just moves the decimal point two places to the left, with a result of 0.12.

49. A: Figure out which is largest by looking at the first non-zero digits. Choice B's first non-zero digit is in the hundredths place. The other three all have non-zero digits in the tenths place, so it must be A, C, D, or E. Of these, A has the largest first non-zero digit.

50. E: $40N$ would be 4000% of N. It's possible to check that each of the others is actually 40% of N.

Dear CBEST Test Taker,

We would like to start by thanking you for purchasing this study guide for your CBEST exam. We hope that we exceeded your expectations.

Our goal in creating this study guide was to cover all of the topics that you will see on the test. We also strove to make our practice questions as similar as possible to what you will encounter on test day. With that being said, if you found something that you feel was not up to your standards, please send us an email and let us know.

We would also like to let you know about other books in our catalog that may interest you.

CSET English

This can be found on Amazon: amazon.com/dp/1628455586

CSET Multiple Subject

amazon.com/dp/1628454504

NES Elementary Education

amazon.com/dp/1628454334

CSET Mathematics

amazon.com/dp/1628454571

We have study guides in a wide variety of fields. If the one you are looking for isn't listed above, then try searching for it on Amazon or send us an email.

Thanks Again and Happy Testing!
Product Development Team
info@studyguideteam.com

Interested in buying more than 10 copies of our product? Contact us about bulk discounts:

bulkorders@studyguideteam.com

FREE Test Taking Tips DVD Offer

To help us better serve you, we have developed a Test Taking Tips DVD that we would like to give you for FREE. **This DVD covers world-class test taking tips that you can use to be even more successful when you are taking your test.**

All that we ask is that you email us your feedback about your study guide. Please let us know what you thought about it – whether that is good, bad or indifferent.

To get your **FREE Test Taking Tips DVD**, email freedvd@studyguideteam.com with "FREE DVD" in the subject line and the following information in the body of the email:

      a. The title of your study guide.

      b. Your product rating on a scale of 1-5, with 5 being the highest rating.

      c. Your feedback about the study guide. What did you think of it?

      d. Your full name and shipping address to send your free DVD.

If you have any questions or concerns, please don't hesitate to contact us at freedvd@studyguideteam.com.

Thanks again!

Made in the USA
San Bernardino, CA
31 July 2019